CURT ERSKINE

Foreword by Bobby Harrington

I0149206

RECREATED

TO

BE LIKE GOD

Making Disciples in the Image of Jesus

A **DISCIPLESHIP.ORG** RESOURCE

DISCIPLESHIP.ORG

Recreated to Be like God: Making Disciples in the Image of Jesus
Copyright © 2022 by Curtis V. Erskine

Requests for information should be sent via email to
info@discipleship.org. Visit Discipleship.org for contact information.

ISBN: 979-8-9864710-0-6 (Paperback)
ISBN: 979-8-9864710-1-3 (Kindle)
ISBN: 979-8-9864710-2-0 (ePub)

Cover and interior design: YouPublish (youpublish.com)

Curtis Erskine identifies the real cure for struggling churches and followers of Jesus. It is to obey and imitate Jesus. He reminds the reader of the importance of the need for disciple making that helps followers of Jesus be transformed into the image of God through four specific principles. Read on if you are in the habit of bringing glory to God through disciple making.

Dr. Carl Williamson, Andy T. Ritchie Jr. distinguished chair for discipleship and church planting, Harding University

In *Recreated to Be like God*, Curtis takes a deep dive into what it means to be a disciple in every aspect of one's life. In a church culture that values attendance over transformation, this book will challenge the reader to examine what they say about discipleship and, more importantly, what their life says about discipleship.

Dan Leitz, lead pastor, Calvary Chapel

In *Recreated to Be like God*, Curt Erskine offers a fresh, solidly biblical understanding of discipleship as it relates to the image of God as the basis of discipleship. This is not just theory. Curt has fleshed it out in his own life and in the lives of his church family. This is an important and helpful book that will sharpen your paradigm for making disciples.

Dave Earley, associate professor of discipleship at Liberty University School of Divinity, lead pastor, First Baptist Church of Grove City

Curtis cuts through the fog of ministry goals and methods to lay out a clear, concise, and compelling case for the bullseye of all our kingdom work. This book is a wake-up call for both growing and stagnant churches. No church—or Christian—is exempt from this central message.

James Brummett, senior pastor, Journey Christian Church

This invaluable guidebook makes it easy to engage youth and young adults in discussions of God's ultimate purpose for people by answering the most pressing questions about truth, life, and identity. This is a highly recommended resource for discussions in small groups!

Jay Manimtim, lead minister, Central Church of Christ, Winnipeg, Manitoba

Recreated to Be like God has a pointed message for the church: become like Jesus by obeying Him and by making disciples of others in a relational environment. Erskine compellingly uses both Scripture and church history to make the case that *this* is what being a Christian is all about. The power of such a focused message could transform the church and you! Don't miss it!

Justin Gravitt, director of innovation and advancement, Navigators Church Ministries

In *Recreated to Be like God*, Curtis does a fantastic job of clearly pointing to what a disciple should look like according to Scripture. Have we confused what the end goal of discipleship is supposed to look like in an individual's life? Curtis answers that question and clearly paints the picture of what a disciple should look like, how we've missed it, and how we get back to the model that the New Testament lays out.

Matt Hessel, lead pastor, LifeBridge
Christian Church

Erskine lays out in a convincing, concise way the vital nature of knowing the goal of disciple making and how this idea of reconstruction into the image of God as we were created to be occurs through obedience to Jesus' teachings and His methods of creating disciples. Erskine gives four practical statements for believers and church leaders to evaluate as they create this paradigm shift in their lives and churches. It is a recommended read.

Michelle Eagle, women's discipleship minister,
Harpeth Christian Church

Curtis Erskine delivers a clear apologetic for the much ignored yet biblically rooted concept of *theosis*. He speaks with authority as he continually points readers to the Word of God, which leave no doubt that we need the image of God restored in us. In sharing this message, he pushes back on the common postmodern assertion that human beings are basically good—and therefore fine just as we are. His primary critique, however, is not targeted at the world, but rather the watered-down teachings that exist in many of our churches. This is a must-read for all those who accurately seek to represent God's hope for humankind: image restoration.

Paul Huyghebaert, church leader, author of *The Way Back: Repentance, the Presence of God, and the Revival the Church So Desperately Needs*

Recreated to Be like God captures an essential truth that is both simple and profound. Obedience is certainly an integral part of disciple making, but Curtis goes beyond suggesting mere compliance. He reaches to the motive of imitating and obeying Christ. His core theme is clear: the aim of true disciple making is about being re-conformed to the image of God. This motivation breathes a fresh incentive into the act of surrender in the journey of disciple making. This is a much-needed word for the church today.

Dr. Steve McCoy, founder, SMALLCIRCLE

ABOUT DISCIPLESHIP.ORG

Discipleship.org is a collaborative community
of men and women committed to the
discipleship lifestyle—being disciples of
Jesus and making disciples of Jesus.
Imagine a day when disciple making is the
norm for the local church! Everyday Christians
engage in relationships with people (inside
and outside the church) so they can show
the love of Jesus and help people to trust and
follow him. Churches are known as disciple-
making places, where Jesus-like people are
created. And pastors are evaluated by the
people they raise up and the disciple makers
they have made in the Spirit's power. Jesus'
message AND Jesus' methods dominate.
If this resonates with you, check out
DISCIPLESHIP.ORG and consider joining
the many church leaders and everyday
disciple makers who join our NATIONAL
DISCIPLE MAKING FORUMS.

To Ronnie, Jeanette, Jessie, Piper, and Vincent. Thank you for putting up with me continually going back to school. This book is the result.

CONTENTS

FOREWORD

Why should the local church focus on disciple making? I am a big advocate of this exact focus, and I have sought to encourage every church leader I can to embrace it through my leadership roles at Discipleship.org and Renew.org, and in the books that I have written.

But why disciple making?

Why advocate for this primary focus?

Two principal reasons are typically given to church leaders, but both are inadequate in of themselves.

The first principal reason is pragmatic. What we are doing is not working, and we need discipleship or disciple making. Christians are starting to realize this truth that the world is out-discipling the church and turning people away from Scripture. Christians must get back to disciple making to counteract the world. They are also starting to realize that church services are not enough. How can only one or two hours on a Sunday counteract the discipling influence of five to seven hours a day of social media and entertainment?

Finding statistics to support this pragmatic argument is easy. Disciple making advocates can point to the latest Barna studies or Gallup studies that show the rapid decline in the influence of the teachings of Jesus, both in the local church and the global church. They note the rapid decline in those who hold to a Christian worldview, a decline in those who consider themselves practicing Christians, and in those who even attend church.

Will Mancini and Cory Hartman make a strong case for the pragmatic argument in their book *Future Church: 7 Laws of Real Church Growth*. They make it clear that the best future of the church is going to be a focus on disciple making. I recommend their book for that reason.

But it is not enough.

The second principal reason is the Great Commission in Matthew 28:18–20, where Jesus teaches us to make disciples.

> Then Jesus came to them and said, "All authority in heaven and on earth has been given to me. Therefore go and make disciples of all nations, baptizing them in the name of the Father and of the Son and of the Holy Spirit, and teaching them to obey everything I have commanded you. And surely I am with you always, to the very end of the age."

"These are the words of Jesus himself," we say. "Making disciples is a commandment. We must obey his command."

Sometimes we rally people to obedience to this command by pointing to Jesus' heart for the world.

"Let's make his last words our first priority," we say. "If Jesus loved the world and taught us to love the world by making disciples of everyone, then we must make it a priority."

I agree with this second reason too.

But it is not enough.

One commandment in isolation, even if it is the Great Commission, is not enough in itself to develop a theology of mission for the local church. To be holistic and show the multifaceted teaching of the New Testament, we need a deeper, more profound theology.

This holistic approach comes through *theosis,* which teaches that God wants everyone *recreated into the image of Jesus.* This underlying theology should make disciple making the core focus of the local church.

A focus on *theosis* will motivate the local church to transform people in the image of Jesus Christ. Properly understood, it makes disciple making a more authentic and a more deeply rooted and all-pervasive mission. It calls every church leader to always be conscious that our goal for everyone in the church is to be like Jesus. It calls us to structure everything and emphasize in everything that this is God's goal for us in the church.

We can describe it simply—God wants everyone to come to salvation in Jesus Christ and to form their entire lives around Jesus Christ. C. S. Lewis put it succinctly:

The Church exists for nothing else but to draw men into Christ, to make them little Christs.

If they are not doing that, all the cathedrals, clergy, missions, sermons, even the Bible itself, are simply a waste of time. God became Man for no other purpose.[1]

Curt Erskine's book is vitally important for us because it makes the biblical and historic case for this focus. Again, a focus on *theosis* emphasizes that God's ultimate goal is for everyone in the local church be recreated into Jesus' image.

Read it thoughtfully and carefully.

May this teaching form your focus on being a disciple and making disciples.

— Bobby Harrington, pastor and CEO,
Discipleship.org and Renew.org

ACKNOWLEDGMENTS

I want to thank Mike Brown for recognizing the importance of being recreated in the image of God and for committing to making sure that this message is heard. Thank you to Bobby Harrington for encouraging me, and to Chad Harrington and Jared Austin for being brutally honest editors. Thank you to Dave Earley for introducing me to being and making disciples of Jesus.

INTRODUCTION

I knew something was wrong, but I couldn't quite put my finger on it. After spending my entire life in the evangelical church, I knew the church wasn't making the impact that it should be making in the lives of believers (including mine). To find the answer, I began studying theology in seminary. While finishing up a master's in theology, I took an elective class on discipleship (being and making disciples of Jesus) that completely changed my life. In forty years of attending church, I had not been taught how to be or make a disciple of Jesus—much less the importance of it.

In that discipleship class I read Putman and Harrington's *DiscipleShift*. As I read through the book, I sat in my living room and alternated between crying from broken-heartedness over the condition of the church and laughing for joy over having finally found what I believed to be the answer for the condition of our churches. I then read the rest of Putman's books and attended a *DiscipleShift* conference at his church to see if what they were proposing was possible.

After the conference, I became convinced that it was. I also became convinced that even though I was a youth pastor, I didn't know how to be or make a disciple of Jesus. So I resigned from my position, moved back to my hometown, got a secular job, and began working toward an MDiv that focused on discipleship ministries.

As I continued to study discipleship, two concepts that I had never considered before consistently stood out in the materials I read. The first concept was that being a disciple of a master is primarily imitating and obeying that master to become like him. *Therefore, being a disciple of Jesus is first and foremost imitating and obeying Him in order to be conformed to His image.*

The second concept was *the ultimate goal of Jesus' gospel is that believers are to be recreated into the image of God that they were originally created to be, and in doing so, render glory unto God by fulfilling their original created purpose.* I honestly had never heard of that concept before. However, in my studies I discovered that the early church fathers, as well as Calvin, Wesley, Bonhoeffer, C. S. Lewis, A. W. Tozer, and others, clearly taught the concept of re-creation into the image of God. More importantly, I discovered the Scriptures clearly teach re-creation into the image of God, especially throughout the New Testament.

Theosis

The church fathers even had a specific Greek term for believers being recreated into the image of God: *theosis.* In more recent history, this word has almost exclusively been used by the Eastern Orthodox Church. However, the modern Eastern Orthodox Church's concept of *theosis* has been somewhat modified from the original concept as taught in Scripture and by the early church fathers. The Eastern Orthodox concept of *theosis* often emphasizes participation in the sacraments of the church as well as keeping the commands of Jesus.

Protestants and evangelicals tend to favor the term "sanctification" to describe the same concept. However, like any word that is unfortunately overused, "sanctification" has (in my opinion) lost its power and meaning in the evangelical church. Like many other biblical words, "sanctification" has become a word we toss around without really understanding what we are saying. This is why I personally use the term *theosis*: most evangelicals are unfamiliar with it, which provides an opportunity to define the concept properly.

Scripture itself doesn't use the word *theosis*, just as it doesn't use the word "Trinity." Instead, the church fathers coined the term *theosis* in the same way they coined the term "Trinity" to describe the Father, Son, and Holy Spirit. Both are abstract concepts clearly laid out in Scripture that the early church clearly accepted. The terms Scripture uses to reference *theosis* are when a believer is "created," "conformed," or "transformed" into the image of Jesus or God. Therefore, for the sake of brevity, I will use the early church fathers' term *theosis* interchangeably with the concept of "believers being recreated into the image of God that He originally created them to be."

So what does *theosis* have to do with being a disciple of Jesus?

Theosis Through Being and Making Disciples of Jesus

One day while writing an outline on discipleship, I realized that if believers are conformed to the image of Jesus through imitating and obeying Him as His disciples, and if Jesus is the perfect image of God, then believers will be recreated into the image of God through imitating and obeying Jesus. Furthermore, as I continued to study discipleship in Scripture, I realized *theosis* through discipleship is more than just an interesting concept; rather, it is a central theme in Scripture.

The outline that I jotted down when I first stumbled onto the idea of *theosis* through discipleship ultimately took this form:

1. *The Image of God as the Basis of Discipleship.* The ultimate goal of the gospel of Jesus (and therefore Christian discipleship) is that believers bring glory to God by being recreated into the image of God that they were originally created to be.
2. *The Purpose of Imitating and Obeying Jesus as His Disciple.* The goal of believers being recreated into the image of God is accomplished by their imitating and obeying Jesus (who is the perfect image of God) as His disciples through the supernatural empowerment and enlightenment of the Holy Spirit.

3. *Jesus-Style Disciple Making.* Imitating and obeying Jesus as His disciple begins (but does not end) with specifically learning and then keeping the words, teachings, commands, and example He gave during His earthly ministry. Someone cannot imitate and obey someone without knowing what they said and did.

4. *Biblical Discipleship in a Relational Environment.* Being conformed to the image of Jesus by imitating and obeying Him as His disciple is not a passive process but an active and interactive process that occurs within a relational environment. Jesus established and demonstrated such a relational environment during His earthly ministry.

Moreover, I believe our failure to teach these points (*theosis* through discipleship in particular) is a significant reason we struggle to be and make disciples of Jesus in the modern evangelical church. Simply stated, if we don't know the end goal of an activity exactly, then we will be confused about how to accomplish it. While I thoroughly believe in discipleship, being and making disciples is not the ultimate end goal of the gospel. Rather, we are to be and make disciples who imitate and obey Jesus so we might bring glory to God by being recreated into the image of God that He originally created us to be. That is the end goal of the gospel of Jesus.

Furthermore, in the absence of teaching re-creation into the image of God through imitating and obeying Jesus as His disciples, many evangelicals have substituted a form of moralistic deism that only requires Christians to believe that Jesus died for their sins and then attempt to be a generally moral person (which is highly subjective). We have failed to teach that disciples of Jesus must be willing to abandon every aspect of their fallen lives to be conformed to the image of Jesus, which is what Jesus and Scripture both clearly teach.

Why Teach *Theosis* Through Discipleship?

To be clear, my point is not merely to teach people the word *theosis*. I only use it because an unfamiliar word can be a good icebreaker that gets people's attention. What matters to me is that evangelicals teach people what the Bible says about how and why they are to be Jesus' disciples. He clearly taught what is required to follow Him as His disciple:

> If anyone comes to me and does not hate . . . even their own life—such a person cannot be my disciple. And whoever does not carry their cross and follow me cannot be my disciple. . . . Those of you who do not give up everything you have cannot be my disciples. (Luke 14:26–27, 33)

If we are going to ask people to "hate their own life, carry their cross, and give up everything" to become a disciple of Jesus, then we probably owe them a good explanation as to why they should do so, what exactly they are giving up, and what exactly they are attempting to achieve.

Stop and think about the ridiculousness of it all: we ask people to abandon everything to imitate and obey Jesus as His disciple without giving them the ultimate goal that Scripture gives. No wonder we struggle to make disciples of Jesus. Teaching *theosis* through discipleship is how we clearly explain why we must abandon our previous lifestyles to be recreated into the image of God. We don't necessarily have to use the term *theosis*; the word isn't important, but the concept is important.

I want to pose this question: If you are convinced that Scripture teaches these principles, but you personally have not been teaching or keeping them, are you willing to admit your failure, and then rectify your failure by beginning to teach and live these principles?

I am not suggesting that we do something new that I came up with. Instead, we must teach principles that both Scripture and the early church taught but that the modern evangelical church has often not taught. Since we have not regularly taught or done these principles in the modern evangelical church, they may seem new.

My purpose, therefore, is to convince you that these four principles both are scriptural and were taught regularly at the inception of the church. Further, our failure to teach and keep these principles in the modern church will partially explain our failure to achieve the success that the early church achieved in being and making disciples for Jesus.

RECREATED TO BE LIKE GOD

You heard about Christ and were taught in him
in accordance with the truth that is in Jesus.
You were taught, with regard to your former
way of life, to put off your old self, which is
being corrupted by its deceitful desires; to
be made new in the attitude of your minds;
and to put on the new self, created to be like
God in true righteousness and holiness.

— EPHESIANS 4:21–24

When I first began to plant a church, I started by teaching the book of Ephesians. I remembered from my New Testament studies that Ephesians may have been a circular letter that was meant to be read by all the early churches in Asia Minor. I figured that if it was a letter meant for all the first-century churches, it would be a good place for us to start as a church.

I had studied Ephesians before, but what was different this time was that as I read and taught through the letter, I did so through the lens of being a disciple of Jesus, just as the early church would have done. In Ephesians 4, Paul segued from the theological concepts of the first half of the letter to the practical instructions for Christian living found in the latter half. In the middle of this transition, Paul wrote something that I had never noticed before in verse twenty-four: "Put on the new self, created to be like God in true righteousness and holiness."

I distinctly remember reading that passage and realizing that Paul wrote "created to be like God" instead of "like Jesus." I was obviously familiar with the concept of believers being conformed to the image of Jesus from verses such as Romans 8:29, but I had never put two and two together. Of course, Jesus is God the Son, whom the Scriptures refer to as the perfect image of God. Therefore, if believers are conformed or recreated into the image of Jesus, then they would also be recreated into the image of God (which is what they were originally created to be).

I sat there stunned and wondered, *Why didn't anyone ever teach me that in church? That makes so much sense.* This was also the first moment I fully realized that we are saved for more than just escaping hell. God saves us to return us to our original state, back to His original design.

Because I was studying discipleship at the time, I also recognized the first sentence of Ephesians 4:21–24 referred to being a disciple of Jesus: knowing and keeping His words, teachings, commands, and example. This then was also the first time I equated being a disciple of Jesus with being recreated into the image of God. Which again, makes complete sense. If as disciples of Jesus we are to be conformed to His image through imitating and obeying Him, and He is the perfect image of God, then the obvious result would be re-creation into the image of God.

This brings me to the first point of that discipleship outline:

The Image of God as the Basis of Discipleship. The ultimate goal of the gospel of Jesus (and therefore Christian discipleship) is that believers bring glory to God by being recreated into the image of God that He originally created them to be.

Over time, I also realized that if the gospel of Jesus is the overall story of the Bible, then the story of Scripture must also be about believers being recreated into the image of God.

Telling the Story That Scripture Tells

Because most human beings love a good story, understanding *theosis* through discipleship is a great way to explain the story of Scripture when conducting evangelism or teaching a new believer. The rest of this chapter explains how to share the gospel with an unbeliever and teach new believers to understand Scripture in light of *theosis*.

When explaining the story of salvation and re-creation, I begin in Genesis with the creation of mankind in the image of God, followed by mankind's fall into sin and the damage it inflicted on the image of God within them. Next, I point out the reality of the curse in human history and that Jesus came not only to pay for the sins of mankind but also to reverse the effects of that curse by recreating believers into the image of God.

I explain that human nature has now been corrupted and we often turn to evil, further distorting the image of God. People can choose one of two sides: the side of evil or the side that strives to overcome evil through imitating and obeying Jesus by the Spirit. I conclude with how Jesus promised to return one day and destroy the evil in the world and completely restore creation along with all those conformed to His image. I leave them with the choice to continue to be a part of fallenness and evil or to become a part of the solution by imitating and obeying Jesus. That is the story Scripture tells, so that is the story I tell.

The Introduction to the Story. The Bible is more than just a book about God. It is a book about God written to humans to explain who God is, what humans are to Him, and the relationship between God and humans. Ultimately, the overall story of the Bible is about *theosis*: how God created humans in His image to bring glory to Himself, how humans fell from that original state, how

Jesus (through both His earthly ministry and His death, burial, resurrection, and enthronement to the right hand of God) came to redeem the image of God within fallen humans, and how believers go through the process of *theosis* until they are completely conformed to His image at their glorification.

In any good story, the introduction to a character often describes their most important attributes. The Bible (the greatest story ever written) is no exception. The Scriptures introduce humans with these words:

> Then God said, "Let us make mankind in our image, in our likeness." . . . So God created mankind in his own image, in the image of God he created them; male and female he created them. God blessed them and said to them, "*Be fruitful and increase in number; fill the earth and subdue it.*" (Gen. 1:26–28)

God gave humans two specific commands: to be fruitful and to subdue creation. God created humans to rule His creation as His image bearers; they were to multiply His image, thereby multiplying His glory across creation.

To this end, the psalmist wrote of human beings:

> What is mankind that you are mindful of them, human beings that you care for them? You have made them a little lower than the angels and crowned them with glory and honor. You made

them rulers over the works of your hands; you put everything under their feet. (Ps. 8:4–6)

Throughout Scripture, the glory of God and His image are connected and often paired. For example, Paul wrote, "[Man] is the image and glory of God" (1 Cor. 11:7). As the image of God, human beings are to reflect and magnify the glory of God to the highest degree. God created humans as the crown jewel and rulers of His creation. Their existence and rule should have brought honor and glory eternally to God as they reflected His perfect nature in a perfect environment. So what happened?

The Conflict. Every good story also has a conflict that drives the plot forward. Genesis 3 introduces the conflict whereby Satan tempted humans to take control of their own destiny by becoming more than just the image of God. The first rule of exegesis is "context, context, context." Satan's temptation of Adam and Eve should be understood in the immediate context of the previous chapters of Genesis. In fact, the whole Bible should be understood in the context of the first few chapters of Genesis where God created human beings in His image, commanded them to multiply and to subdue the earth, and then gave them everything they needed to successfully keep those commands.

In response to humanity's creation in the image of God, Satan tempted Adam and Eve to be something more than the mere image of God, to become equals with God with the ability to determine for themselves what is right and wrong: "You will be like God, knowing good and evil" (Gen 3:5). As usual, a measure of truth accompanied Satan's lies; when Adam and Eve took and ate of the Tree of Knowledge of Good and Evil, they became something other than their original purpose. Ironically, by seizing control of their own lives through tasting the forbidden fruit, Adam and Eve became less like God.

Just as the temptation of the first humans should be understood in the immediate context of their creation in the image of God, the curse on their sin should be understood in this context as well. In the fall, the image of God in humans became marred and broken, and their relationship with God was destroyed. Only within humanity's communal relationship with (and therefore obedience to) God were they able to function as His image bearers. As a result, the two functions that God assigned to humans, multiplying and subduing, were cursed by God.

Through Eve, God cursed the function of multiplication: "I will make your pains in childbearing very severe; with painful labor you will give birth to children" (Gen. 3:16). Through Adam, God cursed humanity's subjugation of the earth: "Cursed is the ground because of you; through painful toil you will eat food from it all the days of your life" (Gen. 3:17). No longer would they be able to render glory to God as His image bearers by multiplying and subduing creation, at least not to the degree for which they were created. Instead, sin and death contaminate everything that humans touch. As Paul wrote, "For all have [missed the mark] and fall short of the glory of God" (Rom. 3:23).

Then God decreed to Satan that a human champion (one who would be the perfect image of God), whose life, death, and resurrection would be the climax of the story, would completely defeat him (and the curse): "I will put enmity between you and the woman, and between your offspring and hers; he will crush your head, and you will strike his heel" (Gen. 3:15).

Meanwhile, since they submitted to Satan's deception rather than God's truth, humans relinquished their dominion of the world system to Satan. The Scriptures call Satan the "god of this world" (2 Cor. 4:4). He temporarily rules the fallen world system through deception and lies, hellbent on destroying God's image bearers and keeping them from being restored into His image and into a relationship with Him.

As the story of Scripture unfolds throughout the Old Testament, we see the curse on multiplication and dominion come to fruition. Childbearing was a double-edged sword. Children disappointed their parents, multiplying their sins and failures. The firstborn son of Adam and Eve murdered the second born. Genesis 5 emphasizes once again that Adam and Eve were created in the image of God, but then Scripture emphasizes their third son, Seth, was born in the image of Adam.

In story after story in the Old Testament, humans struggled against both the land for food and against other humans for control of the land. Rather than worshiping the Creator as His image bearers, mankind worshiped images of creatures as gods. Rather than subjugating the earth through service and work, humans set themselves up as fallen gods to subjugate each other.

The Old Testament tells of kings ruling harshly and warring among themselves for control. This is the rising action and continued conflict of the overall story. Even when God gave the descendants of Abraham the promised land, their sin caused famines and wars to overtake the land. No matter how hard they tried, humans couldn't overcome the curse on their multiplication and dominion.

The Rescuer and Redeemer. In a love story, the climax occurs when the protagonist must rescue his love interest from the grasp of the antagonist. Everything else leads up to this point in the story. In like manner, the New Testament begins with humanity in a deeply fallen state. Satan ruled Western civilization through the Roman Empire. In Asia, Satan ruled through various military kingdoms and dynasties in India, China, and Japan. In South America, early civilizations built temples and worshiped graven images of jungle animals as idols. While on the surface humans appeared to rule the earth, it was only through the subjugation and destruction of other humans. Ironically, the *Pax Romana* ("the peace of Rome") was accomplished through bloodshed, mass crucifixions, and the continued threat of violence.

With Emperor Nero on his throne in Rome, the author of Hebrews quoted Psalm 8:4–6, and then added: "In putting everything under [humans], God left nothing that is not subject to them. *Yet at present we do not see everything subject to them*" (Heb. 2:8). Humans worked in vain throughout history to subjugate creation and maintain relationships but couldn't carry out their original functions as images of God. Instead, they were pawns of Satan, destroying themselves and creation.

Thankfully, the author of Hebrews also wrote:

> *But we do see Jesus, who was made lower than the angels for a little while, now crowned with glory and honor because he suffered death, so that by the grace of God he might taste death for everyone. In bringing many sons and daughters to glory*, it was fitting that God, for whom and through whom everything exists, should make the pioneer of their salvation perfect through what he suffered. (Heb. 2:9–10)

Jesus was the human descendant of Eve who would crush the head of the serpent and overcome the curse. He was "crowned with the glory and honor" that Adam and Even forfeited. Then as the "pioneer of their salvation," Jesus forged the path by which fallen humans would become "sons and daughters" who once again resemble their Father and are crowned with the honor and glory that humans were created to bear.

The author of Hebrews went on to write:

> Since the children have flesh and blood, he too
> shared in their humanity so that by his death he
> might break the power of him who holds the power
> of death—that is, the devil. . . . For this reason he
> had to be made like them, fully human in every
> way, in order that he might become a merciful and
> faithful high priest in service to God, and that he
> might make atonement for the sins of the people.
> Because he himself suffered when he was tempted,
> he is able to help those who are being tempted.
> (Heb. 2:14, 17–18)

In the Old Testament, the high priest stood between God and humans and offered animal sacrifices for the sins of mankind. But those sacrifices were only temporary and symbolic. No matter how pure, an animal could never pay the price of the sins of fallen humans. Only a human could pay the price of humanity's sin, but no human could afford it. Only a human who was also fully God could withstand the penalty. Jesus alone, as both fully man and fully God, could act as mediator between the two and restore the relationship.

Jesus was fully God, and He absorbed mankind's rejection of God when we tortured Him and nailed Him to a cross. Jesus was also fully human as God the Father unleashed His full rejection of mankind on Him as He hung on the cross. As the fully divine, fully human God-man, Jesus alone absorbed the omnipotent wrath of God against the sin of humanity: "Pierced for our transgressions, crushed for our iniquities, the punishment that brought us peace was on him" (Isa. 53:5).

As He hung between God and mankind, both physically and spiritually, Jesus absorbed their rejection toward one another as He cried out, "Father, forgive them, for they do not know what they are doing," (Luke 23:34) and, "My God, my God, why have you forsaken me?" (Matt. 27:46). But our forgiveness is not automatic. Human beings must enter a union with Jesus to be shielded from the wrath of God toward their sin. Otherwise, they will stand before Jesus one day having rejected Him, tortured Him, crucified Him, and having had the weight of their sins laid upon Him.

Hebrews 2 lists Jesus' two purposes: that His death might make atonement for the sins of humans, but also that His life might free them from the bondage of sin and help them overcome temptation. This is important because for far too long we have taught in evangelical churches that Jesus only came to pay for our sins and thereby purchase us a free trip to heaven. Scripture, however, is clear that Jesus also came to free us from the bondage of sin in the here and now. But how does He do that as a high priest?

The Rescue Plan. The author of Hebrews explains Jesus' role as a high priest and how it plays a part in our rescue. The job of the high priest in the Old Testament was not only to offer sacrifices for sins but also to be a leader and moral guide to the people. He was responsible for teaching them to know and keep the law of God (Lev. 10:8–11). Not only does Jesus stand between the Father and humanity as a mediator, but He is also the perfect example of the image of God that humans are to imitate and obey.

Moreover, Jesus is a "high priest in the order of Melchizedek." In Genesis 14, Melchizedek was more than a high priest: he was the king of Salem, which is most likely the original name of Jerusalem (Ps. 76:2). Jesus is the only true king of humanity and should be obeyed as such.

The author of Hebrews wrote:

> Son though he was, he learned obedience from what he suffered and, once made perfect, *he became the source of eternal salvation for all who obey him* and was designated by God to be high priest in the order of Melchizedek. (Heb. 5:8–10)

The source of eternal salvation for whom? This might be one of those times when you need to check if you really believe "all Scripture is God-breathed and is useful for teaching" (2 Tim. 3:16). Because as much as it goes against the grain of American Christianity, we must recognize that biblical Christianity requires those who "believe" in Jesus also to be willing to abandon all in order to imitate and obey Him as His disciple—or they do not believe in Him. You can call it legalism if you want, but you must give an answer as to why Scripture and Jesus both agree that those who don't obey Him don't know Him.

The apostle John (who knew Jesus better than any of us) wrote:

> We know that we have come to know [Jesus] if we keep his commands. Whoever says, "I know him," but does not do what he commands is a liar, and the truth is not in that person. But if anyone obeys his word, love for God is truly made complete in them. This is how we know we are in him: Whoever claims to live in him must live as Jesus did. (1 John 2:3–6)

So why must we imitate and obey Jesus as His disciples if His death on the cross paid for our sins?

We find the answer as we continue to follow the story of the image of God through Scripture. Multiple times the Scriptures refer to Jesus as "the image of God." For example:

- "The Son is the image of the invisible God, the firstborn over all creation" (Col. 1:15).
- "The god of this age has blinded the minds of unbelievers, so that they cannot see the light of the gospel that displays the glory of Christ, who is the image of God" (1 Cor. 4:4).
- "The Son is the radiance of God's glory and the exact representation of his being" (Heb. 1:3).

Nothing is random or accidental in Scripture. Jesus being identified as "the image of God" alludes back to mankind's original purpose as the image bearers of God. Jesus is the image of God that Adam failed to be. From there the math is simple. If humans imitate and obey Jesus (who is the perfect image of God), then they will become the images of God that He originally created them to be and thereby render unto God the glory He is due. Thus, through both Jesus' death and life, humans can be restored to their original purpose.

In and through Jesus, the two lovers in the story who were separated, God and humanity, are reconnected. Not only through Him can humans be forgiven of their sins, but also through Him can humans regain their relationship with God. This is the story of Scripture: God rescuing His true love, His image bearers, from the deception and destruction of Satan, thereby restoring them to their original purpose. This is why Jesus came as a human being.

Our Part in the Plan. Jesus taught, "A disciple is not above his teacher, but everyone who is fully trained will be like his teacher" (Luke 6:40, CSB). Notice that a disciple who is "fully trained" is conformed to the likeness of his teacher. Therefore, a disciple of Jesus must enter into training to be conformed to His image. Even in 2 Timothy 3:16, Paul wrote that Scripture is good for "training in righteousness." Previously, Paul had told Timothy to "train [himself] to be godly," just as one commits to physical training (1 Tim. 4:5–8). A disciple of a rabbi in the first century would have trained to be like his master in every way possible. The point of training to imitate and obey Jesus as His disciple is to become like Him, the image of God.

To this end, most of the New Testament books have either an allusion or a direct reference to believers being conformed to the image of Jesus. This is a vital point to note. Paul wrote: "And we all, who with unveiled faces contemplate the Lord's glory, are being transformed into his image with ever-increasing glory, which comes from the Lord, who is the Spirit" (2 Cor. 3:18), and, "You have taken off your old self with its practices and have put on the new self, which is being renewed in knowledge in the image of its Creator" (Col. 3:9–10). These are typical passages from the New Testament. Disciples are not passive participants but actively strive to imitate and obey Jesus and become like Him.

Jesus also taught, "This is to my Father's glory, that you bear much fruit, showing yourselves to be my disciples" (John 15:8). Therefore, by imitating and obeying Jesus as His disciple and by multiplying disciples who do the same, humans now render glory unto God as they were originally created to do. They fulfill the command to be fruitful and multiply the image of God across the face of creation by being and making disciples of Jesus.

The Conclusion of the Story. Like many good stories, the Bible bookends. In the opening, we see God and humans in the garden in a perfect state. In the conflict, humans betrayed God, lost their ability to serve as His image bearers, and were separated from Him. In the climax, Jesus the hero came and rescued mankind, making a way for humans to once again become the image of God they were originally created to be. And then in the conclusion, as seen in the final chapter of Scripture, the last vision of humanity shows them free from the curse and once again bearing the image of God perfectly, ruling and reigning over creation in a relationship with Him.

As John wrote:

> Then he showed me the river of the water of life, clear as crystal, flowing from the throne of God and of the Lamb down the middle of the city's main street. The tree of life was on each side of the river, bearing twelve kinds of fruit, producing its fruit every month. The leaves of the tree are for healing the nations, *and there will no longer be any curse.* The throne of God and of the Lamb will be in the city, and his servants will worship him. *They will see his face, and his name will be on their foreheads.* Night will be no more; people will not need the light of a lamp or the light of the sun, because the Lord God will give them light, *and they will reign forever and ever.* (Rev. 22:1–5)

But what did John mean by, "They will see his face, and his name will be on their foreheads" and "there will no longer be any curse"? In his first epistle, John also wrote, "We know that when Christ appears, we shall be like him, for we shall see him as he is. All who have this hope in him purify themselves, just as he is pure" (1 John 3:2–3). At our glorification, the "curse" on mankind's functions as the image of God from Genesis 3 will be lifted and the process of re-creation will be complete when we see Jesus face to face. We will finally, perfectly, and completely reflect His image.

But we don't wait until then to be conformed to His image. Notice that John also wrote, "All who have this hope in him purify themselves, just as he is pure." If believers look forward to the day when they will be completely conformed to His image, then they begin that process now by imitating and obeying Jesus as His disciples.

The Scriptures show the kingdom of God as a kingdom where humans, as the image of God, rule through work and service. This is the kingdom that Jesus came to reestablish and restore. In that sense, Jesus' kingdom is a kingdom of re-creation. One day He will return to recreate the heavens and the earth back into the perfect paradise He originally created them to be. However, the first order of business is to recreate the people who will inhabit that paradise for all eternity. For our part, we either choose to be a part of the kingdom by being recreated into His image here and now, or we choose not to participate and enter that kingdom neither now nor then.

How Did We Miss It?

In mid-twentieth-century America, A. W. Tozer was one of evangelicalism's greatest preachers and forward thinkers. Yet much of what he preached and wrote over sixty years ago sounds as if he were addressing today's evangelical church. Moreover, he was adamant that *theosis* was the end goal of the gospel of Jesus. He preached:

> The purpose of God is not to save us from hell; the purpose of God is to save us and make us like Christ and to make us like God. God will never be done with us until the day we see His face, when His name is on our foreheads; and we shall be like Him because we shall see Him as He is.[2]

He also wrote:

> For worship to be acceptable to God, you must be renewed after the image of Him that created you. That "image" must be restored. Only the renewed man can worship God in a way worthy of and acceptable to Him. . . . This is the purpose of redemption: taking on the material of fallen man and by the mystery of regeneration and sanctification, restoring it again so that he is like God and like Christ. This is why we preach redemption. That is what redemption is; it is not saving us from hell, although it does save us from hell; but more importantly, it is making it so that we can be like God again.[3]

When I first read those quotes from Tozer, I wondered, *How did evangelicals miss it?* Tozer is well-known, well-respected, and well-quoted. I had heard of Tozer often in college, but I had never heard of being recreated into the image of God. Only after forty years in church and a chance elective class on discipleship did I even begin to consider the concept. Moreover, not only did Tozer emphasize *theosis* but also other well-known theologians and preachers did so as well. How did we miss them all saying the same thing? More importantly, *theosis* through discipleship is clearly taught in Scripture. How did we miss that?

Because we have missed this important aspect of Scripture, we have not been telling people the whole story. To be and make disciples of Jesus as they did in the early church, we must return to teaching everything Scripture teaches just as they did in the early church. The Bible begins and ends with mankind being created and then recreated into the image of God for a reason. The recurring themes of the image of God, graven images in the Old Testament, and the image of Jesus in the New Testament are there for a reason. The Bible tells a beautiful story about the relationship between man and God—we should tell the same story.

But please don't take my word for it. In the next chapter, I will explore more Scripture and historical examples of the church teaching *theosis* through discipleship as well as how we missed it. I will point out scriptures in addition to those we have already covered that support the concept of believers being recreated into the image of God. From there, I will begin with the examples of the church fathers teaching *theosis*. Then I will follow the thread to the modern church. Finally, I will look at why I believe we neglected teaching *theosis* through discipleship and what it will cost us to begin to do so again.

2

SCRIPTURAL AND HISTORICAL SUPPORT

Be perfect, therefore, as your
Father in heaven is perfect.
— MATTHEW 5:48

There is a quote I have heard often that is attributed to Billy Graham but originated with Charles Spurgeon: "If you find a perfect church, don't join it because you will mess it up." The original Spurgeon quote is a little deeper but basically expresses the same sentiment. More recently, I have seen advertisements on Facebook for sermon series titled something like "No Perfect People Allowed." I have joked with my wife that the mission statement for many churches should be, "Nobody is perfect, so don't worry about it."

While I understand the point being made, what concerns me is that Jesus commanded His disciples to "be perfect" just as God is perfect. Somehow, someway, we must understand what Jesus is asking of His disciples and come to terms with it. I'm not saying that I expect people to be perfect either (at least not until their glorification). But as a disciple of Jesus, I want to keep the command of my Master. I want to understand what He is asking of me. Surely, I can't be the first person who wondered what Jesus meant when He commanded us to be perfect as God is perfect. Surely something in Scripture and church history explains what Jesus asks of us.

After I noticed that Paul wrote "created to be like God" in Ephesians 4:24 and that Scripture clearly teaches *theosis*, I realized I might have actually read of the concept before. I started looking back through a few of the discipleship books I owned and finally found it in Bonhoeffer's *The Cost of Discipleship*:

> The image of God should be restored in us once again. This task encompasses our whole existence. The aim and objective is not to renew human thoughts about God so that they are correct, or that we would subject our individual deeds to the word of God again, but that we, with our whole existence and as living creatures, are the image of God. Body, soul, and spirit, that is, the form of being human in its totality, is to bear the image of God on earth. God is well pleased with nothing less than God's own perfect image.[4]

When people discuss Bonhoeffer's *The Cost of Discipleship*, the conversation usually revolves around the concepts of cheap grace versus costly grace. This is understandable given the gravity of the implications for the church and the kingdom of God. However, what has often been neglected in the conversation is Bonhoeffer's conclusion as to the ultimate purpose of following Jesus as His disciple. In the final chapter, Bonhoeffer argued that the chief end of the gospel is that people bring glory to God by being recreated into the image of God that He originally created them to be.

I remember rereading that final chapter and thinking, *Bonhoeffer should have led with that. Everything else makes so much more sense in light of that.* Honestly, my mind was so blown by everything else Bonhoeffer wrote about discipleship that by the time I got to the final chapter I couldn't retain any more information. As a result, when I began outlining how to be a disciple of Jesus, I took my own advice and led with this principle.

Scriptural Support

To be clear though, Bonhoeffer was not the first person to write this principle down; he pulled it straight from Scripture. In addition to Ephesians 4:24, the apostle Paul also wrote:

- "And we all, who with unveiled faces contemplate the Lord's glory, are being transformed into his image with ever-increasing glory, which comes from the Lord, who is the Spirit" (2 Cor. 3:18).
- "You have taken off your old self with its practices and have put on the new self, which is being

renewed in knowledge in the image of its Creator" (Col. 3:9–10).

Conformity to the image of Jesus requires that the old, fallen self be abandoned and crucified. Moreover, this is only accomplished through the power and the presence of the Holy Spirit.

As you can see below, Paul consistently wrote in his epistles about being conformed to either the image of Jesus, God, or both:

- "For those God foreknew he also predestined to be conformed to the image of his Son, that he might be the firstborn among many brothers and sisters" (Rom. 8:29).
- "Therefore be imitators of God, as beloved children" (Eph. 5:1).
- "Be imitators of me, just as I also am of Christ" (1 Cor. 11:1).

(See also Gal. 2:20; 1 Cor. 15:49; Phil. 3:10–11; Col. 2:9–10; 1 Thess. 1:6; Titus 3:4–6.)

But this concept isn't confined to the writings of Paul; Peter's first epistle likewise focuses on believers being like Jesus (1 Pet. 1:3). Moreover, the author of Hebrews (12:1–2), James (1:4), and the apostle John (1 John 3:2–3) all allude to believers being conformed to the image of Jesus or God. John wrote it perhaps the most directly: "In this world we are like Jesus" (1 John 4:17).

But did Jesus ever teach us to be recreated into the image of God? Perhaps the best example is when Jesus commanded His disciples, "Be perfect, therefore, as your heavenly Father is perfect" (Matt. 5:48). That verse is perhaps one of the most important, and equally most dismissed, verses in the Bible. I have literally been in a Bible study where the leader's only comment on that verse was, "Of course, no one is perfect," and then he moved right along to the next verse. We don't get to dismiss the commands of Jesus that easily. However, until I understood *theosis* through discipleship, I had no idea how to keep that command either. Now, in light of the rest of the Scriptures that teach being recreated into the image of God, I understand that Jesus commanded His disciples to imitate God as His image bearers and children, just as Paul did in Ephesians 5:1.

Another teaching of Jesus that is either grossly ignored or misinterpreted is John 10:34–35 where He quoted Psalm 82:6: "I said, 'You are "gods"; you are all sons of the Most High.'" Thus, Jesus commanded His disciples to be recreated into the image of God by referring to an Old Testament passage that also states: "Defend the weak and the fatherless; uphold the cause of the poor and the oppressed. Rescue the weak and the needy; deliver them from the hand of the wicked" (Ps. 82:3–4). Believers are to be recreated into the image of God through treating people how Jesus treats people.

Scripture consistently teaches not only that believers are to be recreated into the image of God, but also how we are to do so: by imitating and obeying Jesus. Again, John went as far as to write that if we fail to imitate and obey Jesus as His disciples, then we are liars and do not know Him:

> We know that we have come to know [Jesus] if we keep his commands. Whoever says, "I know him," but does not do what he commands is a liar, and the truth is not in that person. But if anyone obeys his word, love for God is truly made complete in them. This is how we know we are in him: Whoever claims to live in him must live as Jesus did. (1 John 2:3–6)

I also place this passage high on the list of "too easily dismissed." Stop and think for a minute about what would happen if we took that passage seriously in our churches and held members to that standard. Either they are disciples of Jesus who are in the process of learning to imitate and obey Him or they are liars who do not know Him. How many church members would you lose teaching that? But this truth is in the Bible, and evangelicals must teach the Bible.

Historical Support

I am wary when people say Scripture taught them something I have never heard before. Generally, there is no new theology. If something hasn't been taught historically by the church, then there is probably a reason it

Recreated to Be like God

hasn't been taught. So as I began to explore *theosis* and how it relates to imitating and obeying Jesus as His disciple, I was pleasantly surprised to find that re-creation in the image of God was taught regularly by famous church leaders, thinkers, and theologians.

Jesus famously alluded to *theosis* in His object lesson using a Roman coin. Caesar stamped his image on Roman coins to signify their value, his ownership of them, and his authority over commerce. When Jesus stated, "Give back to Caesar what is Caesar's and to God what is God's" (Mark 12:17), He taught that just as Caesar could exert ownership of those coins and demand they be returned to him through taxes, human beings on whom God had stamped His image should rightfully be restored to Him.

You might think, *I have never heard that. I have always heard the passage was about believers having to pay taxes.* First, yes, believers should pay their taxes. But the real point of that story was that Jesus dismissed what everyone thought was the most important question of the day (Should Jews should pay taxes to Rome?) and instead pointed them to the most important problem in human existence: humans are not the image of God that He created them to be. Rather than trying to sort out if they should pay taxes, believers should focus on imitating God and being recreated into His image. Then they will easily know if they are supposed to pay taxes or not.

You might also think, *If that is how this passage is supposed to be taught, then why have I never heard that?*

It's the same reason you have never heard of being recreated into the image of God through imitating Jesus as His disciple. However, some of the earliest teachings of the church on Jesus using the example of the coin clearly taught *theosis*. Tertullian, a theologian who converted from paganism in the early third century, wrote concerning this teaching of Jesus:

> [Render] the image of Caesar, which is on the coin, to Caesar, and the image of God, which is on man, to God; so as to render to Caesar indeed money, to God yourself.[5]

Ignatius, an early church father who was most likely discipled by John the apostle, also commented in the early second century:

> For as there are two kinds of coins, the one of God, the other of the world, and each of these has its special character stamped upon it. . . . The unbelieving are of this world; but the believing have, in love, the character of God the Father by Jesus Christ.[6]

In fact, an unbroken legacy of *theosis* being taught throughout the early history of the church exists, beginning with the authors of the New Testament in the first century, and then it was picked up immediately by church fathers such as Irenaeus, who purportedly met John the apostle. Irenaeus clearly taught *theosis*:

Recreated to Be like God

> For in times long past, it was said that man was created after the image of God. . . . Wherefore also he did easily lose the similitude. When, however, the Word of God became flesh. . . . He reestablished the similitude after a sure manner, by assimilating man to the invisible Father through means of the visible Word.[7]

Clement, a theologian in the second century who had converted from paganism, wrote that through conformity to Jesus, believers are recreated into the image of God that He originally created them to be:

> He Himself formed man of the dust, and regenerated him by water; and made him grow by his Spirit; and trained him by His word to adoption and salvation, directing him by sacred precepts; in order that, transforming earth-born man into a holy and heavenly being by His advent, He might fulfil to the utmost that divine utterance, "Let Us make man in Our own image and likeness." And, in truth, Christ became the perfect realization of what God spake; and the rest of humanity is conceived as being created merely in His image.[8]

Athanasius of Alexandria was the great defender of the Trinity against Arianism. He wrote extensively on *theosis* in the early fourth century while defending the concept of the Trinity, and his explanation of *theosis* is perhaps the most famous among the church fathers. He compared mankind to a self-portrait painted by God that had been damaged by the weather. Because the artist valued His own image and His own creation, He was compelled to restore the painting to its original condition:

> For as, when the likeness painted on a panel has been effaced by stains from without, he whose likeness it is must needs come once more to enable the portrait to be renewed on the same wood, for the sake of his picture, even the mere wood on which it is painted is not thrown away, but the outline renewed upon it; in the same way also the most holy Son of the Father, being the image of the Father, came to our region to renew man once made in his likeness, and find him, as one lost, by the remission of sins.[9]

Gregory of Nyssa lived in the fourth century as well. He wrote that believers are conformed to the image of God when they dwell on Jesus and imitate Him through the power of the Holy Spirit that dwells within them:

> The sky was not made in God's image, not the moon, not the sun, not the beauty of the stars, no other things which appear in creation. Only you were made to be the image of nature that surpasses every intellect, likeness of incorruptible beauty, mark of true divinity, vessel of blessed life, image

of true light, that when you look upon it you become what He is, because through the reflected ray coming from our purity you imitate He Who shines within you, . . . He dwells in you and moves within you without constraint, saying that "I shall live and walk for them." (Lev. 26.2)[10]

Basil of Caesarea was Gregory's older brother. Like Athanasius, he defended the Trinity against Arianism, and like his brother and Athanasius, he clearly taught *theosis*:

For what is set before us is, so far as is possible with human nature, to be made like God.[11]

Augustine of Hippo lived in the fourth and fifth centuries. He is not only a revered Catholic theologian, but he also had a great influence on the Reformation with his teachings on grace. He likewise taught that *theosis* is the end goal of the gospel as promised in Scripture:

We carry mortality about with us, we endure infirmity, we look forward to divinity. For God wishes not only to vivify, but also to deify us. When would human infirmity ever have dared to hope for this, unless divine truth had promised it?[12]

The greatest gap in teaching *theosis* by the church occurred during the "dark ages" of the medieval Roman Catholic Church, but it returned with the Reformation.

Interestingly though, *theosis* was not exclusive to any Protestant theological leanings. For instance, John Calvin wrote clearly that *theosis* was the end goal of the gospel:

> Since the image of God had been destroyed in us by the fall, we may judge from its restoration what it originally had been. Paul says that we are transformed into the image of God by the gospel. And, according to him, spiritual regeneration is nothing else than the restoration of the same image. . . . Hence, too, we learn, on the one hand, what is the end of our regeneration, that is, that we may be made like God, and that his glory may shine forth in us; . . . Paul, at the same time, teaches, that there is nothing more excellent at which the Colossians can aspire, inasmuch as this is our highest perfection and blessedness to bear the image of God.[13]

John Wesley was an Anglican priest and the founder of the Methodist movement. Theologically, he was Arminian; however, he agreed with Calvin on *theosis*. Wesley preached:

> Man knows not that he is a fallen spirit, whose only business in the present world, is to recover from his fall, to regain that image of God wherein he was created.[14]

Recreated to Be like God

C. S. Lewis is perhaps the most practical and relatable twentieth-century Christian theologian. His famous book *Mere Christianity* began as a series of lectures on the BBC during World War II because he intended to present Christian theology in a manner that was understandable to the public. Interestingly, Lewis's conclusion on the ultimate goal of the gospel has also often been overlooked. Lewis clearly argued in *Mere Christianity* that God's goal is to restore believers back to their original form in order to reflect His glory. Moreover, Lewis recognized *theosis* was a process that occurred in this life:

> The command "Be ye perfect" is not idealistic gas. Nor is it a command to do the impossible. He is going to make us into creatures that can obey that command. He said (in the Bible) that we were "gods" and He is going to make good His words. If we let Him—for we can prevent Him, if we choose—He will make the feeblest and filthiest of us into a god or goddess, dazzling, radiant, immortal creature, pulsating all through with such energy and joy and wisdom and love as we cannot now imagine, a bright stainless mirror which reflects back to God perfectly (though, of course, on a smaller scale) His own boundless power and delight and goodness. The process will be long and in parts very painful; but that is what we are in for. Nothing less. He meant what He said.[15]

Notice Lewis's conclusion: "That is what we are in for. Nothing less. He meant what He said." *Theosis* through discipleship is Christianity. There is not another version of Christianity where believers do not have to be recreated into the image of God through imitating and obeying Jesus as His disciple—not unless it is a false Christianity.

Modern Evangelicalism

Clearly, *theosis* as the end goal of being and making disciples of Jesus is not only taught in Scripture but was also taught throughout the history of the church. So I must raise the question again: How did we miss it? Three of the most well-known twentieth-century Christian thinkers (Bonhoeffer, Lewis, Tozer) in some of their most famous books argued that *theosis* was the end goal of the gospel of Jesus, but not until I went looking for the concept did I discover it had been taught by great men of God throughout church history.

Ever since then, I have consistently watched to see how often *theosis* is taught in modern evangelicalism. I've observed that re-creation to the image of God is only occasionally mentioned in evangelical circles as the end goal of imitating and obeying Jesus as His disciples. One of the newest, most popular Christian books on the image of God, *In His Image* by Jen Wilkin, touches on the subject:

> God's will is that the cracks in the image we bear be repaired so that we represent him as we were

created to do, so that we grow to look more and more like our brother, Christ, in whom form and function displayed themselves flawlessly. "He is the image of the invisible God, the firstborn of all creation" (Col. 1:15). As such, he serves as both our model and our guide: "For to this you have been called, because Christ also suffered for you, leaving you an example, so that you might follow in his steps" (1 Pet. 2:21). And as the apostle John points out, "Whoever says he abides in him ought to walk in the same way in which he walked" (1 John 2:6). If we want to look like him, we will walk as he walked. . . . God's will for our lives . . . shows itself to those who have learned to ask, "Who should I be?" and look to the person of Christ for their answer. It shows itself to those whose deepest desire and dearest delight is to be remade—in his image—one carefully placed step at a time.[16]

Likewise, Matthew Bates has written in *The Gospel Precisely* that restoration in the image of God is the goal of Christian discipleship:

Disciple making highlights this point. Its goal is to help everyone conform to Jesus' image, as we reflect God's glory through the Spirit. Paul describes the purpose of his disciple-making ministry in 2 Corinthians 3:2–3 as crafting "living letters" written by the Spirit. He then describes the end result for disciples: transformation "into his image with ever-increasing glory, which comes from the Lord, who is the Spirit" (2 Corinthians 3:18). . . .

Paul concludes his remarks about the human problem in Romans 3:23 with his famous words: "All have sinned and fall short of the glory of God." Notice that even though it is true that we are unrighteous, he does not say, "All have sinned and fall short of God's perfect standard of righteousness." Rather, Paul speaks about the lack of God's glory.

Paul wants to remind us that salvation is about more than a personal falling short of God's holy standard. We need the restoration of human image-bearing, so that everyone and everything in creation will no longer lack God's glory. Then God will be glorified by his creatures. This focus helps us to remember that our goal in the local church is spirit-empowered disciple making, which transforms everyone more and more into the image of King Jesus.

We all need good news about a king because creation needs the restoration of proper human rule. God intends humans to carry his image to creation, so it can experience his glory. But image-bearing has become distorted by sin. We need a flawless human king who can restore God's glory amid humanity's brokenness. Then creation can be ruled by humans properly again and God can receive the glory that is his due.[17]

Therefore, one can't say that *theosis* is never taught in the modern American evangelical church. However, one can argue it is not taught regularly, clearly, and in every evangelical church in America. Why is this?

The evangelical church has spent much of the last century engrossed in battles within Christendom over the exclusivity of Jesus and the inerrancy and inspiration of Scripture and in battles outside of Christendom over the culture at large. This is not to argue these are not battles worth fighting, but amid these battles the American evangelical church forgot the goal of Christendom.

Over the last 150 years, the American evangelical church rediscovered the academic understanding of imitating and obeying Jesus as His disciple. This journey seems to have begun with Scottish author A. B. Bruce's *The Training of the Twelve* (1871). From there, the concept flowed through several different authors and ended up as the relational discipleship concept that is currently growing popular in the American evangelical church.

However, while American evangelicalism rediscovered that believers are called to be disciples of Jesus, the importance of why believers are to imitate and obey Jesus as His disciples has not been emphasized. As relational discipleship is being promoted, there is some pushback, which raises the questions: "Why should we engage in relational discipleship? Isn't it enough that we believe that Jesus died for our sins?" Often the answer is "Because Jesus said so." This is a true statement, but it fails to answer *why* Jesus said so.

Therefore, to maintain the momentum of disciple making in modern American evangelicalism, we must teach what Scripture clearly teaches (which should be reason enough): that the end goal of being and making disciples of Jesus is to bring glory to God by being recreated into the image of God that He originally created them to be. The early church made disciples of Jesus by teaching *theosis* through discipleship; therefore, the modern church should do the same.

What About the Cost?

Another reason we haven't consistently taught *theosis* through discipleship in the modern evangelical church is the cost. How many church members would we lose if we taught something new? How many more would we lose if we taught that if they don't imitate and obey Jesus then they are probably not saved (as Scripture clearly teaches)? Most importantly, what would it cost you personally to imitate and obey Jesus?

I can't necessarily answer the first two questions, but I can answer the last question: it will cost you your fallenness. The cost of imitating and obeying Jesus and being recreated into the image of God is everything about you that is not like Jesus. The cost of *theosis* through discipleship is the fallen you.

The problem is that the fallen you is all you have ever known, and you have to crucify that individual in order for the real you, the you that was created in the image of God, to be reborn. That is a scary proposition: to sacrifice what you have always believed to be the real you for something you have never known. But the new you will be like Jesus. You will love like Jesus. You will give like Jesus. You will sacrifice like Jesus. One day, you will rule with Jesus.

Conversely, the fallen you is a contributor to the woes of the world and must be crucified for its sins. Bonhoeffer wrote:

> Human beings have lost their own, God-like essence, which they had from God. They live without their essential purpose, that of being the image of God. Human beings live without being truly human. They must live without being able to live. That is the paradox of our existence and the source of our woes.[18]

While the cost of *theosis* may seem high, think of the cost of not imitating and obeying Jesus—remaining the fallen you who isn't even truly human. Is that a price you are willing to pay? Are you willing to sacrifice the true you for the false you? More importantly, are you going to refuse to render unto God the glory He is due by refusing to be recreated into His image?

The cost of *theosis* through discipleship is high, but the lie of Satan is that the cost of not being recreated into the image of God is somehow less. This is the same lie that deceived Eve. So how do we make the choice to eat of the Tree of Life instead of the Tree of the Knowledge of Good and Evil? The simple answer is to make the choice to imitate and obey Jesus as His disciple. But what does that truly mean? In the next couple of chapters, we will look at what it means to be the disciple of a first-century rabbi who claimed to be the Son of God.

3

IMITATING AND OBEYING JESUS

In this world we are like Jesus.

— I JOHN 4:17

I grew up in a church setting where being a Christian meant believing Jesus died for your sins, being a fairly moral person, and being a political and theological conservative. I can only remember one time in Sunday school that someone vaguely said something about being like Jesus. In all those years in church, how is it that I can only remember one distinct time that I was sort of taught that I was supposed to be like Jesus?

In contrast, I can remember plenty of times that I was taught to keep our traditions and defend our denomination. I can remember being taught to be a good person, but I can also remember being taught racist jokes and discrimination against the poor. What they considered being a "good person" was subjective to the surrounding culture. My tradition taught us to believe the Bible but then conveniently ignored passages that confronted the sins of our culture. Worse yet, they took other passages out of context to justify those same sins.

By God's grace, I really believed in Jesus, and when they taught me to read my Bible on my own, I listened. Even in the archaic language of the one translation we were told to read, I could understand that there were passages and commands of Jesus that we weren't keeping. Unfortunately, if I brought those up, the response I received was generally something like, "Well, nobody is perfect. Just be a good person."

But that is the point. Imitating and obeying Jesus as His disciple is more than just being a good person. Even an unbeliever can be a good person by the standards of the culture around them. Imitating and obeying Jesus requires the supernatural empowerment and enlightenment of the Holy Spirit. Imitating and obeying Jesus requires a commitment to know and keep His commands and example. And it is only through imitating and obeying Jesus as His disciple that we render unto God the glory He is due. Therefore it is important that we accurately understand what it means to be a disciple of Jesus.

When I wrote that original discipleship outline (mentioned in the beginning), I attempted to make each point logically flow from the previous point. If disciples of Jesus are to be conformed to the image of God, they should next find out how to do that. Therefore, the second point of that outline and the next scriptural principle we have failed to teach in the modern evangelical church is:

The Purpose of Imitating and Obeying Jesus as His Disciple. The goal of believers being recreated into the image of God is accomplished by their imitating and obeying Jesus (who is the perfect image of God) as His disciples through the supernatural empowerment and enlightenment of the Holy Spirit.

While any believer would (hopefully) agree that they should imitate and obey Jesus, most typically can't answer exactly *why* they should. Believers generally miss the connection between imitating and obeying Jesus and being recreated into the image of God.

Also, the last part of that principle comes up quite often when I speak to people about *theosis* through discipleship: Isn't it the Holy Spirit's responsibility to conform us to the image of Jesus? The verse most often cited to support this thought is: "For it is God who works in you to will and to act in order to fulfill his good purpose" (Phil. 3:18). Unfortunately, as with many Bible passages, we tend to focus on one part of the verse without considering the entire verse. We like to emphasize the first and last part of the verse: "It is God who works in you . . . in order to fulfill his good purpose," while skipping the middle part: "to will and to act."

The Holy Spirit changes us by supernaturally empowering and enlightening us "to will and to act." But to what purpose does the Holy Spirit empower and enlighten us "to will and to act"? The obvious answer is the Holy Spirt empowers and enlightens us to imitate and obey Jesus as His disciples.

Paul also wrote:

> And we all, who with unveiled faces *contemplate the Lord's glory*, are being transformed into his image with ever-increasing glory, *which comes from the Lord, who is the Spirit.* (2 Cor. 3:18)

What does it mean to "contemplate the Lord's glory"? It would seem strange to say that anyone who sits around and thinks about God's glory will be conformed to His image.

An exegetical tip to better understand the New Testament epistles is to remember that they were mainly written to people who already understood exactly what it meant to be a disciple of Jesus. Therefore, they would have understood "contemplating the Lord's glory" in terms of being a disciple of Jesus. It meant studying and contemplating the teachings, commands, and example of their Lord with the intent of imitating and obeying Him.

Another exegetical tip is to look beyond the artificial chapter and verse breaks in modern Bibles. They weren't there originally and occasionally interrupt complete thoughts. If we continue reading 2 Corinthians 4,

Paul continued the thought he began in the third chapter and further explained what it means to "contemplate the Lord's glory":

> And even if our gospel is veiled, it is veiled to those who are perishing. The god of this age has blinded the minds of unbelievers, so that they cannot see the light of the gospel that displays the glory of Christ, who is the image of God. For what we preach is not ourselves, but Jesus Christ as Lord, and ourselves as your servants for Jesus' sake. For God, who said, "Let light shine out of darkness," made his light shine in our hearts to give us the light of the knowledge of God's glory displayed in the face of Christ. (2 Cor. 4:3–6)

Notice that the gospel specifically displays "the glory of Christ" as "the image of God." Moreover, the gospel that Paul preached was "Jesus Christ as Lord." You cannot call Jesus "Lord" unless you are willing to obey His commands and teachings (which would include imitating Him). Finally, notice that believers shine with the "light of the knowledge of God's glory displayed in the face of Christ." Therefore, it is impossible to shine with that knowledge unless we have spent time contemplating Jesus through knowing and keeping His words, teachings, commands, and example that He gave during His earthly ministry.

I have heard a statement multiple times from the pulpit of well-meaning evangelical churches in reference to the Holy Spirit's empowering Christians: "It's a mystery. He changes you from the inside out." Again, that statement is well-meaning but incredibly vague and, in my opinion, unhelpful.

Will the Holy Spirit really transform me into the image of Jesus no matter what I do? Even if I don't go to church or study Scripture or fellowship with other believers? I can just sit on the couch at home, and the Holy Spirit will "mysteriously" transform me into the image of God? Most of us don't truly believe that, but we say it because we don't know what else to say.

Jesus, however, taught concerning the empowerment and enlightenment of the Holy Spirit:

> If you love me, keep my commands. And I will ask the Father, and he will give you another advocate to help you and be with you forever—the Spirit of truth. . . . Whoever has my commands and keeps them is the one who loves me. . . . Anyone who loves me will obey my teaching. My Father will love them, and we will come to them and make our home with them. Anyone who does not love me will not obey my teaching. . . . The Advocate, the Holy Spirit, whom the Father will send in my name, will teach you all things and will remind you of everything I have said to you. (John 14:15–17, 21, 23, 26)

Jesus clearly taught that one of the main purposes of the Holy Spirit is to empower and enlighten believers to be

Recreated to Be like God

able to remember the words, teachings, and commands He gave, and then to be able to keep them. Conversely, a lack of desire to keep them would signify an absence of the Holy Spirit.

Not Salvation by Works

The debate is not as to whether the Holy Spirit powers the transformation, but rather the amount of work involved on our part due to our Protestant distaste for salvation by works. The passage evangelicals quote most often when arguing against salvation by works is Ephesians 2:8–10:

> For it is by grace you have been saved, through faith—and this is not from yourselves, it is the gift of God—not by works, so that no one can boast. For we are God's handiwork, created in Christ Jesus to do good works, which God prepared in advance for us to do.

However, that passage also clearly teaches that believers are saved to be "created in Christ Jesus to do good works." In light of the rest of Scripture, those "good works" for which believers have been "created in Christ Jesus to do" are clearly imitating and obeying Jesus as His disciple.

Paul wrote that Scripture is useful for "training in righteousness, so that the servant of God may be thoroughly equipped for every good work" (2 Tim. 3:17).

Again, the "good works" for which the Scriptures equip believers should be understood as imitating and obeying Jesus as His disciples. To the Romans, Paul wrote, "Through him we received grace and apostleship to call all the Gentiles to the obedience that comes from faith for his name's sake" (Rom. 1:5). To what are believers called? Obedience to Jesus!

Obviously, we are not saved by works, but we are saved to accomplish the works of imitating and obeying Jesus as His disciples. We are not only being saved from the penalty of our sin, but we also are being saved from our fallenness, our inability to be the image of God. We are being saved that we might render glory unto God through being recreated into His image. Finally, one day we will be completely recreated into His image and exist in that state for all eternity in a recreated paradise.

Therefore, believers do not go through this life reveling in their fallenness, waiting until judgment day to be conformed to the image of Jesus. Instead, the re-creation begins now when believers imitate and obey Jesus as His disciples through the supernatural empowerment and enlightenment of the Holy Spirit.

Be Perfect?

If you could pick a verse from the Sermon on the Mount to be the thesis of the sermon, what would you choose? I know what I would pick: "Be perfect, therefore, as your heavenly Father is perfect" (Matt. 5:48). Everything else in the Sermon on the Mount is about how to do that. But can we reach perfection before we step into paradise?

Another helpful rule of exegesis is to "let Scripture interpret Scripture." In Philippians, Paul uses the same Greek word for "perfect" that Jesus used in the Sermon on the Mount:

> Not that I have already reached the goal or am already perfect, but I make every effort to take hold of it because I also have been taken hold of by Christ Jesus. Brothers and sisters, I do not consider myself to have taken hold of it. But one thing I do: Forgetting what is behind and reaching forward to what is ahead, I pursue as my goal the prize promised by God's heavenly call in Christ Jesus. . . . In any case, we should live up to whatever truth we have attained. Join in imitating me, brothers and sisters, and pay careful attention to those who live according to the example you have in us. (Phil. 3:12–14, 16–17, CSB)

Paul realized he had not reached perfection and would not reach it until he stepped into paradise, but he still aimed for perfection through imitating and obeying Jesus as His disciple. An athlete such as Steph Curry is the best example of this principle. When he steps onto the basketball court, Steph Curry clearly attempts to play the perfect game, knowing he never will. But in attempting to play the perfect game, he becomes a better basketball player than the other men who are bigger and more athletic.

Likewise, we should attempt to render as much glory unto God as we possibly can by attempting to imitate and obey Jesus as close to perfection as we possibly can. Moreover, in aiming for the perfection of Jesus, we prepare for that day when we will step across the threshold of paradise and the process of *theosis* will finally be complete. As Paul also wrote to the church at Philippi:

> Our citizenship is in heaven, and we eagerly wait for a Savior from there, the Lord Jesus Christ. He will transform the body of our humble condition into the likeness of his glorious body, by the power that enables him to subject everything to himself. (Phil. 3:20–21, CSB)

Like Paul, I therefore believe that the perfection of Jesus is the goal toward which we continuously strive to become as much like Him as possible in this fallen world.

Judgment Day

If you are saved, and you have the presence of the Holy Spirit, why would you not want to imitate and obey Jesus as His disciple here and now? Conversely, if you do not have the desire to be conformed to His image here and now by imitating and obeying Him as His disciple (and thereby rendering unto God the glory He is due), why do you believe that you will be conformed to His image and allowed into His presence on judgment day?

Jesus clearly taught concerning the storm that will befall many on that day:

> Not everyone who says to me, "Lord, Lord," will enter the kingdom of heaven, but only the one who does the will of my Father who is in heaven. Many will say to me on that day, "Lord, Lord, did we not prophesy in your name and in your name drive out demons and in your name perform many miracles?" Then I will tell them plainly, "I never knew you. Away from me, you evildoers!" Therefore everyone who hears these words of mine and puts them into practice is like a wise man who built his house on the rock. The rain came down, the streams rose, and the winds blew and beat against that house; yet it did not fall, because it had its foundation on the rock. But everyone who hears these words of mine and does not put them into practice is like a foolish man who built his house on sand. The rain came down, the streams rose, and the winds blew and beat against that house, and it fell with a great crash. (Matt. 7:21–27)

Whose lives will withstand the storm of that day? Those who not only hear what Jesus said and taught but also are willing to obey everything He taught. And whose lives will fall with a great crash on that day? Those who hear His words, and perhaps even agree with them, but fail to obey them.

It seems extremely odd to me that we would ask people to devote their entire lives to the enterprise of disciple making without telling them the goal of that enterprise. It seems even odder that we would send them headlong into judgment day without telling them what Jesus said would be asked of them on that day.

Teaching *theosis* through discipleship not only gives the disciples we are making measurable goals toward which to strive, but it also prepares them to enter paradise. While we will never be completely like Jesus until the day we step into paradise, we can become more like Him every day in the here and now, and then be prepared to stand before Him on that day.

To be honest, I wish someone would have taught me those things when I was a young believer. Understanding *theosis* through discipleship would have transformed my life and saved me a lot of grief. By the same token, people in churches deserve to know why they are being asked to devote their entire lives to being and making disciples of Jesus.

As I wrote earlier, another reason a pastor might not want to teach *theosis* through discipleship to his congregation is that he believes members of the congregation will reject the message. This is a valid concern. However, if Scripture teaches *theosis* through discipleship and if members of our congregation reject it, then that is no different than them rejecting any other portion of

Scripture. Just as pastors do not shy away from other controversial teachings in Scripture out of fear of their congregations, they should not shy away from this one either.

Granted, we must be mindful of how well we teach *theosis* through discipleship. With that in mind, this book offers an outline for teaching re-conformity into the image of God through imitating and obeying Jesus as His disciple. Beyond that, the power of the Holy Spirit empowers and enlightens a pastor who is committed to teaching everything Scripture teaches. I cannot imagine sending a congregation of people to stand before Jesus on judgment day without properly preparing them and warning them of the gravity of that day.

The Job Ahead

Paul wrote in Ephesians that God gave pastors and other church leaders as gifts to the church "to equip his people for works of service, so that the body of Christ may be built up until we all reach unity in the faith and in the knowledge of the Son of God and become mature, attaining to the whole measure of the fullness of Christ" (Eph. 4:12–13). Therefore, church leadership must teach the members of a church to imitate and obey Jesus to be conformed to His image.

This will require teaching the Holy Spirit's role in *theosis* through discipleship. It will require church leaders explaining to the congregation why imitating and obeying Jesus as His disciple is not salvation by works. A pastor will have to answer this question more than once: "How can we be like Jesus? Wasn't He perfect?" But the leaders of a church must also be sure to warn its members of the dangers of refusing to imitate and obey Jesus as His disciple.

But a pastor also needs to understand what to do when people agree to imitate and obey Jesus. Say a person walked up to you today and said, "Teach me to be a disciple of Jesus. I don't care what it costs." What would you tell them? In the next chapter we will look at where we should start in the Bible if we want to be a disciple or make a disciple of Jesus.

4

JESUS-STYLE DISCIPLE MAKING

Discipleship is the process of becoming
who Jesus would be if He were you.

— DALLAS WILLARD

I grew up going to church in a well-populated area, but we were theologically isolated due to the church traditions that reigned supreme in the culture. This was partly due to being raised in a church culture that deemphasized seminary at the time. Much was often made of how some of the first apostles were "unlearned and ignorant men" (Acts 4:13, KJV). However, we need to make sure we understand that verse in the correct context.

First, "unlearned" and "ignorant" are probably not the best translations of the Greek words into modern English. Second, the apostles were "unschooled, ordinary men" only by the standards of the members of the Sanhedrin who interviewed them. By modern standards, the apostles were likely bilingual, literate, had much of the Old Testament memorized, and most importantly, had the equivalent of a seminary education from having studied directly under Jesus for three to four years. Acts 4:13 even makes the point that the members of the Sanhedrin "were astonished and they took note that these men had been with Jesus." To us, the apostles would be educated men.

However, because of the theological isolation and distrust of a seminary education, we were steered away from some of the great Christian authors and theologians. I never heard of Bonhoeffer, Tozer, Lewis, Packer, Coleman, Willard, or others even though I grew up in a Christian culture and went to church multiple times a week. This is partly why I was so bewildered when I began to study discipleship. I can remember hearing about Bonhoeffer for the first time in college and wondering why I had never heard of him before.

One of the most shocking things I discovered was the number of people who wrote about being a disciple of Jesus and what it meant to be a disciple of Jesus. As a result of having experienced my own ignorance of discipleship, I know that when I personally share what it means to be disciple of Jesus, I must be exact. Therefore, the third point I wrote down in my outline on discipleship (as listed at the beginning) was a continuation of the second point, and it explains exactly what being a disciple of Jesus requires:

Jesus-Style Disciple Making. Imitating and obeying Jesus as His disciple begins (but does not end) with specifically learning and then keeping the words, teachings, commands, and example He gave during His earthly ministry. Someone cannot imitate and obey someone without knowing what they said and did.

This third principle is important to establish because this is real-world application of being a disciple of Jesus. Being a disciple of Jesus is becoming an expert on what Jesus said and did, and then working to become an expert at doing what Jesus said and did. There is simply no way around it.

Imagine that Jesus came down from heaven, switched places with you, and lived your life. He looked and sounded just like you so that no one knew it was Him; in fact, others thought it was still you. Jesus lived with your family, worked at your job, and dealt with your problems. That is what your life should look like if you're a disciple of Jesus. You should speak to your wife and kids the way Jesus would speak to your wife and kids. You should interact with people at work the way Jesus would interact with your coworkers. You should spend your money (really His money) the way Jesus would spend your money.

Now imagine what it would be like to be around people who acted like Jesus. Wouldn't that be great?

Why wouldn't you want to be one of those people? Is it not in your family's best interest for you to treat them how Jesus would treat them? Is it not in your coworkers' best interest for you to treat them how Jesus would treat them? When problems arise in your life, is it not in your best interest to handle them how Jesus would handle them? To be able to do those things, you first need to know what Jesus would do in those situations. You need to know what He said and did in His own life.

Do You Know What Jesus Said and Did?

I distinctly remember what my childhood best friend told me when I talked to him about being a disciple of Jesus. He said in a slow, Southern drawl, "I know what Jesus said and did." Less than a year later, he stated in the middle of a study of the Gospels, "I had no idea what Jesus said and did." How can we know how to imitate Jesus if we have no idea what He said and did?

I am not the first person to argue that discipleship should begin with Jesus. I am simply agreeing with multiple others who have argued this same point. For example, Dallas Willard stated:

> I say this over and over to people, to pastors, "Just start with Matthew and just preach what Jesus preached." Now that's going to really jerk you around. You have to avoid things like going to your church and saying, "We're going to keep doing things the same but now we're going to really mean

it." That's really what they think, but as long as they do that they're really going to get nowhere. Spiritual formation, as a hope, will flame out within just a few years unless people understand that they really are doing something different than they've done before. So, I say to anyone who asks, "What do we do?" I just suggest that you just start and teach what Jesus taught and begin to put your own life into it and progressively you will see people respond. It will take a little while to realize that you really are saying and doing something different. Then when they do that you'll see various reactions, just like the Parable of the Sower.[19]

[A pastor] should focus his preaching on the Gospels. One should begin preaching what Jesus preached. I would plan to spend two years just preaching from the Gospels. Remember, the gospel as Jesus brought it to earth is the most powerful thing that has ever hit the world. If you preach what he preached, you will see it beginning to pop around you. And you'll find your people asking the right questions: How about this blessing those who curse you? How about loving your enemies? Can we really do that?[20]

In churches, we often assume people know what Jesus said and did. But as pastors and disciple makers, have we ensured the disciples we are making know what Jesus said and did? How can we teach them to imitate and obey Him if we have not personally taught what He said and did? Moreover, have we ensured they understood how what He said applies to them? Have we ensured they understand how to imitate His life?

Dave Earley, one of my professors at Liberty University, introduced me to the concept of being and making disciples of Jesus. Earley personally had a radical awakening to what it means to be a disciple of Jesus. Even though he was the discipleship director at Liberty, he didn't truly understand what being a disciple of Jesus meant until he focused on the words, teachings, commands, and example that Jesus gave during His earthly ministry. He wrote:

> For the last three years, I have been reading the words of Jesus every day. Frankly, it is messing up my life. It is turning much of what I thought, believed in, valued, and dreamed inside out. During this time, I have been asking myself some tough questions. I challenge you to ask yourself the same questions:
>
> Do you even know everything Jesus commanded? If someone held a gun to your head and handed you a sheet of paper and a pencil, could you write down everything Jesus commanded?
>
> Are you really obeying everything Jesus commanded? Are there some commands you avoid because they are too difficult? Have you made

excuses for why you are not doing everything Jesus commanded?

Have you taught your "disciples" to obey everything Jesus commanded? Do they know what He commanded, and are they living it out?

For the Twelve, the call to discipleship was a call to immerse their lives in the words of Jesus. . . . Could it be that a forgotten element of discipleship is that, while not ignoring the rest of Scripture, the fruit-bearing disciple focuses especially on the words of Christ? . . . As we read, study, memorize, and meditate on the words of Jesus, the Holy Spirit will use them to cut us with conviction.[21]

After reading that passage from Earley, I began studying the Gospels in depth, attempting to memorize and keep everything Jesus said and did, and it had the same effect. Even though I had spent my entire life in church and had read through the Bible multiple times, I didn't know what Jesus had said, taught, and done. Moreover, I couldn't differentiate between what Jesus said and what Moses, David, or Paul wrote.

The Starting Point

Of course, this is not to argue against the inspiration and usefulness of the rest of Scripture. This is merely an argument for where to begin teaching in Scripture when making disciples of Jesus (you must begin somewhere).

As stated, I completely agree that "All Scripture is God-breathed and is useful for teaching, rebuking, correcting and training in righteousness, so that the servant of God may be thoroughly equipped for every good work" (2 Tim. 3:16–17).

But at the same time, we are not making disciples of Scripture; rather, we are making disciples of Jesus. And unfortunately, it is entirely possible to believe in a monotheistic God and in large portions of the Bible and still be unwilling to abandon all to imitate and obey Jesus as His disciple. The Bible is a big book with a lot of information; as such, it can be cherry-picked to make disciples of all kinds of different things.

Something often overlooked is that the Pharisees also made disciples of themselves using Scripture in relational environments (Matt. 23:15; Mark 2:18; Luke 5:33; Acts 22:3). Even today, cults make disciples using the Bible. Likewise, many churches use the Bible to make disciples of errant theologies, traditions, worship styles, pastors, denominations, and everything else. They then also employ the logical fallacy of equivocation to label their disciples as "disciples of Jesus," even though they are disciples of something else.

Initially focusing on the words, teachings, commands, and example of Jesus when making disciples forces us to make disciples of only Him. But this raises the question: Is there biblical support for focusing on the teachings of Jesus first?

Whenever Christ spoke of the Old Testament (the only existing Scriptures at the time), He referred to it as "the Law and the Prophets," "Moses and the Prophets," "the Scriptures," "the commands of God," and "the word of God" (Matt. 22:40; Mark 7:8–13; Luke 10:26; 16:29–31; John 5:39–46).

So if Jesus used these terms to refer to Scripture, what does "My words," "My teachings," and "My commands" refer to? Would His original audience have understood Him to mean Scripture (the Old Testament), or would they have understood Him to mean the words, teachings, and commands He spoke during His earthly ministry?

Casting aside presuppositions, the most logical answer is that His disciples would have understood Him to mean the words, teachings, and commands He spoke during His earthly ministry. Those listening to Him would have not yet understood that He was God in human flesh; moreover, the most logical way for Him to refer to the teachings of His earthly ministry would have been to refer to them as "My words," "My teachings," and "My commands."

This is also true in the first-century context of a Jewish rabbi making disciples. A disciple of a first-century rabbi would have sought to memorize and live out every single word their master spoke; further, the word "disciple" in the New Testament appears in the same context every time. Therefore, that is what the word still means today.

The Greek word translated as "disciple," *mathitís*, was a specific word spoken during a specific time in which it had a very specific meaning. We do not get to redefine *mathitís* to advantageously mean whatever we think it should mean today. We are either a *mathitís* seeking to imitate and obey our master by memorizing and keeping the words, teachings, commands, and example He gave during His earthly ministry, or we are not. We are either making *mathitís* by "teaching them to obey everything" Jesus commanded (Matt. 28:20), or we are not.

Did Jesus Refer to His Own Teachings?

One thing that surprised me when I began re-reading what Jesus taught and did in the Gospels was how often He referenced what He said earlier. For example:

> If you love me, keep my commands. . . . Whoever has my commands and keeps them is the one who loves me. . . . Anyone who loves me will obey my teaching. . . . Anyone who does not love me will not obey my teaching. These words you hear are not my own; they belong to the Father who sent me. All this I have spoken while still with you. But the Advocate, the Holy Spirit, whom the Father will send in my name, will teach you all things and will remind you of everything I have said to you. (John 14:15, 21, 23–26)

Notice that Jesus made it clear that He was referring to the words, teachings, and commands He spoke during His earthly ministry. Moreover, Jesus stated one of the purposes of the Holy Spirit was to enable His disciples to remember everything He had said.

Jesus again emphasized the importance of His words: "The words I have spoken to you—they are full of the Spirit and life" (John 6:63). The same is true with:

> If anyone hears my words but does not keep them, I do not judge that person. For I did not come to judge the world, but to save the world. There is a judge for the one who rejects me and does not accept my words; the very words I have spoken will condemn them at the last day. For I did not speak on my own, but the Father who sent me commanded me to say all that I have spoken. I know that his command leads to eternal life. So whatever I say is just what the Father has told me to say. (John 12:47–50)

You might conclude that Jesus constantly emphasized the words, teachings, and commands He spoke during His earthly ministry. If so, you are correct: this is exactly what Jesus did. The Gospels abound with verses that emphasize the spoken words of Jesus. Moreover, Jesus also focused on what He physically did since being a disciple requires a disciple to imitate their master in every way possible:

> But blessed are your eyes because they see, and your ears because they hear. For truly I tell you, many prophets and righteous people longed to see what you see but did not see it, and to hear what you hear but did not hear it. (Matt. 13:16–17)

If disciples of Jesus are to imitate and obey Him, and Jesus emphasized His words and actions, then disciple makers should also emphasize His words and actions to future disciples.

The Greatest Christian Conference Ever

Imagine if you could go to a conference where you could hear some of the major biblical characters and authors speak. However, because of time constraints, they would all be speaking at the same time in separate meeting halls, and you could only pick one individual to listen to. You could listen to Moses explain creation and the flood, David sing the Psalms, Solomon display his wisdom, Daniel explain his visions, Paul explain his theology, John describe his visions in Revelation, or you could listen to Jesus. To whom would you listen?

I hope you said Jesus because based on the passage above, I seriously doubt any of those men would dare speak at the same time as the King of kings and the Lord of lords. They would all be on the front row listening to Jesus.

But at the same time, disciples can't only know the words of Jesus. They must know the rest of the Bible. At

Recreated to Be like God

least two of Jesus' commands require us to know and apply the entire Bible. If we know and keep all His commands, then sooner or later we will also need to know and apply the rest of Scripture as well. Jesus taught:

> Do not think that I have come to abolish the Law or the Prophets; I have not come to abolish them but to fulfill them. For truly I tell you, until heaven and earth disappear, not the smallest letter, not the least stroke of a pen, will by any means disappear from the Law until everything is accomplished. Therefore anyone who sets aside one of the least of these commands and teaches others accordingly will be called least in the kingdom of heaven, but whoever practices and teaches these commands will be called great in the kingdom of heaven. (Matt. 5:17–19)

> Therefore every teacher of the law who has become a disciple in the kingdom of heaven is like the owner of a house who brings out of his storeroom new treasures as well as old. (Matt. 13:52)

Ultimately, focusing on the words, teachings, commands, and example of Jesus does not diminish the need to know and apply all of Scripture—it increases it! Jesus clearly warned His disciples not to set aside the Old Testament, stating that those who did would "be called least in the kingdom of heaven."

Again, I recommend beginning with the direct teachings of Jesus, but not to focus on them solely. Jesus taught His disciples also to focus on the Old Testament and the teachings of the other books in the New Testament. Ultimately, they are all the teachings of Jesus combined. As I demonstrated earlier, the Bible is one cohesive story about God and His relationship with mankind. Jesus' teachings must be understood within that overall story. Jesus taught, and His disciples understood Him, in the context of the Old Testament. After all, both Jesus and the apostles considered the Old Testament to be the inspired, inerrant Word of God. While most of the teachings of Jesus are plain and understandable to all, certain nuances only make sense within the context of the Old Testament. Therefore, the mature disciple of Jesus will need to know the Old Testament to understand and keep the teachings of Jesus completely.

Additionally, the teachings of the apostles in the New Testament are important in that they teach and demonstrate how the church is to keep the initial commands and teachings of Jesus. Moreover, Luke wrote in the book of Acts that the early church "devoted themselves to the apostles' teaching" (Acts 2:42). Therefore, the early church considered the teachings of the apostles to be the teachings of Jesus. This is logical since the apostles were commanded to teach everything Jesus had commanded in the Great Commission.

Furthermore, Jesus taught the apostles that "the Advocate, the Holy Spirit, whom the Father will send

Recreated to Be like God

in my name, will teach you all things and will remind you of everything I have said to you" (John 14:26). This implies the Holy Spirit would not only remind them of Jesus' teachings but also teach them additional information. Given that the Holy Spirit is also referred to as "the Spirit of Jesus" (Acts 16:7; Phil. 1:19; Gal. 4:6), then the teachings of the Holy Spirit are also the teachings of Jesus.

Even though Paul was not among the original apostles, he wrote several times that he had received his teachings directly from the resurrected Jesus (1 Cor. 11:23; 2 Cor. 12:1; Gal. 1:11–12; Eph. 3:3–4). Therefore, the teachings of Paul should be considered the teachings of Jesus as well. Too many "red letter" Christians think that Matthew's rendition of Jesus is superior to Paul's (or that Paul's doesn't have the same degree of inspiration and authority). The point of focusing on the teachings of Jesus as found in the Gospels first is largely a matter of chronological order. The teachings of Jesus in the rest of the New Testament are a continuation of His teachings from the Gospels.

Paul wrote that those who wish to imitate Jesus should imitate him as he imitated Jesus (1 Cor. 11:1; Phil. 3:17). Therefore, those who seek to imitate Jesus today should look to the teachings and example of the apostles as to how they imitated Jesus in the first century. As I wrote previously in this chapter, being a disciple of Jesus begins—*but does not end*—with knowing and keeping the words, teachings, commands, and example of Jesus given during His earthly ministry.

To the Glory of God

Just as we cannot imitate and obey Jesus as His disciples without knowing what He said and did, we also cannot bring glory to God by being recreated into the image of God without knowing and keeping what Jesus said. Imitating Jesus requires replacing our words and our ways with His words and His ways; to do that, we first must know all His words and His ways.

Dallas Willard wrote:

> The crucial thing is that, as disciples, we have a plan for carrying out the decision we have made to devote ourselves to becoming like our Master and Lord—to increasingly live in the character and power of Christ. Disciples are those who, seriously intending to become like Jesus from the inside out, systematically and progressively rearrange their affairs to that end, under the guidance of the Word and the Spirit. That is how the disciple lives.[22]

The simplest first step then, in a plan to bring glory to God by imitating and obeying Jesus as His disciple, is committing to know and keep the words, teachings, commands, and example He gave during His earthly ministry. Afterward, I would recommend focusing on the rest of the New Testament, and eventually studying the Old Testament in depth.

From there, the next step is to make disciples who imitate Him: "This is to my Father's glory, that you bear much fruit, showing yourselves to be my disciples" (John 15:8). Just as God commanded Adam and Eve to multiply and fill the earth with humans who brought glory to God by reflecting His image, Jesus also commanded His disciples to recreate more disciples in His image who bring glory to Him. To this end, Jesus specifically commanded us:

> Therefore go and make disciples of all nations, baptizing them in the name of the Father and of the Son and of the Holy Spirit, and teaching them to obey everything I have commanded you. (Matt. 28:19–20)

We simply cannot teach someone to obey everything Jesus commanded without first teaching them everything Jesus commanded. Further, we cannot teach someone everything Jesus said without having a substantial knowledge of the words, teachings, commands, and example Jesus gave during His earthly ministry.

Training to Be like Jesus

As stated, believers are conformed to the image of Jesus not only by obeying Him but also through imitating Him. This imitation of Jesus has been called different things at times, including "the spiritual disciplines of Christ." As Paul famously wrote, "And we know that in all things God works for the good of those who love him, who have been called according to his purpose" (Rom. 8:28). Paul went on to place that statement in context, "For those God foreknew he also predestined to be conformed to the image of his Son, that he might be the firstborn among many brothers and sisters" (Rom. 8:29). Logically then, God works through the imitation of Jesus to conform believers to Christ's image.

Thus, when Paul told Timothy that he should "train [himself] to be godly" (1 Tim. 4:7), he was admonishing Timothy to commit himself to the spiritual and physical practices that result in being recreated into the image that God created Timothy to be. As Jesus taught, "It is enough for the disciple that he become like his teacher" (Matt. 10:25), and "A disciple is not above his teacher, but everyone who is fully trained will be like his teacher" (Luke 6:40). A "fully trained" disciple, then, is one who imitates their master, which is why Paul commanded Timothy to "train himself to be godly."

But what specifically are the spiritual disciplines of Jesus? Various lists of activities have been composed, including Bible intake, prayer, worship, evangelism, serving, stewardship, fasting, silence and solitude, journaling, and learning. Again, spiritual disciplines at their core must be actions that imitate Jesus. Any action that can be gleaned from studying the life of Jesus is a spiritual discipline that must be imitated.

Moreover, Jesus clearly observed these spiritual disciplines in the community of His disciples, who were the proto-church. The writer of Hebrews also reinforced that spiritual maturity occurs within the community of the church:

> Let us consider how to stimulate one another
> to love and good deeds, not forsaking our own
> assembling together, as is the habit of some, but
> encouraging one another; and all the more as you
> see the day drawing near. (Heb. 10:24–25)

While God provided the spiritual disciplines of Jesus and the Holy Spirit to ensure the re-creation of believers, the community of the church is an equally important facet that produces spiritual maturity. Again, Jesus and the apostles demonstrated this throughout the New Testament. Gathering with other disciples to spur each other on is a spiritual discipline.

The Disciple-Making Rhythms of Jesus

Disciples not only imitate Jesus to be conformed to His image, but they also imitate Jesus to make more disciples in the same way He did. At Discipleship.org, we point to what we call the "Disciple-Making Rhythms of Jesus."[23] During His earthly ministry, Jesus modeled seven recurring, relational rhythms with the twelve men He invited to follow Him. Jesus made disciples who were:

- Grounded in and flowing from *fasting* and *praying* in relationship with His heavenly Father.
- Actively loving people and *inviting along* those who *welcomed* Him into their lives to love others together.
- *Serving* with those He invited along.
- *Eating* and debriefing with those He invited along.
- *Resting/Sabbathing* and retreating and resting with those He invited along.
- *Learning* and living the gospel of His kingdom with those He invited along in all these relational rhythms.
- *Maturing* them *while multiplying* with Jesus to one day send them off to make disciple makers too.[24]

THE 7 DISCIPLE-MAKING RHYTHMS OF A LIFE WITH JESUS

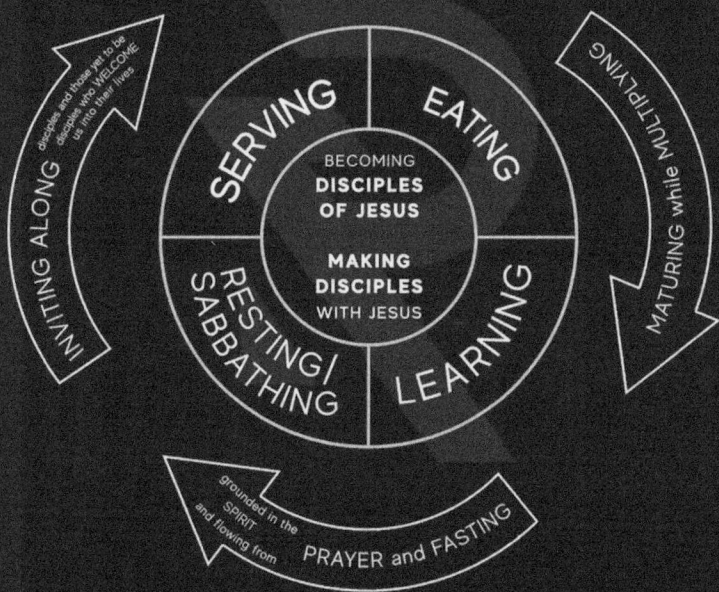

SERVING

EATING

BECOMING
**DISCIPLES
OF JESUS**

**MAKING
DISCIPLES**
WITH JESUS

RESTING/
SABBATHING

LEARNING

INVITING ALONG — disciples and those yet to be disciples who WELCOME us into their lives

MATURING while MULTIPLYING

grounded in the SPIRIT and flowing from PRAYER and FASTING

CREATED BY JASON C. DUKES WITH BOBBY HARRINGTON

Keeping these spiritual disciplines of Jesus is a form of training by which a disciple is conformed to His image. As a disciple purposely keeps these disciplines, they become conditioned to act like Jesus on a regular basis. The more a disciple practices the spiritual disciplines of Jesus, the more natural it becomes for them to act like Jesus as they walk through life. Progressively, disciples of Jesus become less of their fallen selves and more of the new people recreated to be like God.

A first-century disciple of a master or rabbi would have focused on their master's words and actions. A disciple's primary goal would have been to replace their words and ways with their master's words and ways, thus becoming a copy of their master. Thus, understanding and teaching *theosis* through discipleship explains why it is so important to imitate and obey Jesus as His disciple. As His disciples imitate and obey Him, they become conformed to His image, which is the image of God that He originally created them to be. Most importantly, through being recreated into the image of God, disciples of Jesus then begin to render glory once again unto God by fulfilling their original purpose and design.

5

DISCIPLE MAKING THROUGH RELATIONSHIPS

Then [Jesus] looked at those seated in a circle
around him and said, "Here are my mother
and my brothers! Whoever does God's will
is my brother and sister and mother."

— MARK 3:34–35

Every Wednesday night when I was a kid, I attended RAs at my home church (Royal Ambassadors for Christ, a church program like Boy Scouts before there was Awana). And every Wednesday, we rushed through the lesson so we could go outside and play softball. If you had asked me what we did on Wednesday nights at church, I would've said we played softball.

Except we didn't play softball. We usually didn't have enough people to play a game of softball, so we played money-ball. In money-ball you receive an imaginary dime for catching a ground ball, a quarter for a one-hop, and a half-dollar for a fly ball. Whoever reaches an imaginary dollar first gets to bat next.

If you had driven by the church softball field, you would have thought we were playing softball. And if you had asked us, we would have said we were playing softball. But we were not doing the most important thing you do when playing softball: trying to score runs. Everything else revolves around that one goal. If you are not trying to score runs, you are not playing softball; you are just doing something that looks like playing softball.

Softball or Money-Ball

As churches, we often do the equivalent of playing money-ball. We do everything but the one thing we are supposed to be doing: making disciples of Jesus who know and keep all His words, teachings, commands, and example in relational environments. We might insist we are making disciples of Jesus, and to the outside world it might look like we are making disciples of Jesus. But if you look closely at the lives of these supposed disciples, they don't imitate and obey Jesus as His disciples.

Those Wednesday night sessions were a form of relational discipleship, but they didn't teach us to be disciples of Jesus. Some of those guys I played money-ball with are still some of my best friends thirty years later. We developed a lasting, meaningful relationship on those nights. At the same time, if the church had wanted to use those Wednesday nights to teach us to be disciples of Jesus, we would have been there just the same—and probably eager to learn how to be His disciples.

We were usually also at church for Sunday School, the Sunday morning worship service, Sunday night youth group, and then sometimes on Friday or Saturday nights for youth gatherings. We literally "did life together." And in every one of those meetings, someone taught the Bible.

But even though we "did life together" and studied the Bible, no one taught us to be disciples of Jesus. Instead, leaders taught us to be disciples of our traditions, our denomination, our culture, our worship style, etc. The point is that Christians can do relational discipleship and still not make disciples of Jesus. This is why we must establish the other three principles of discipleship that I argued for when we gather together for relational discipleship.

Again, those principles are:

The Image of God as the Basis of Discipleship. The ultimate goal of the gospel of Jesus (and therefore Christian discipleship) is that believers bring glory to God by being recreated into the image of God that He originally created them to be.

The Purpose of Imitating and Obeying Jesus as His Disciple. The goal of believers being recreated into the image of God is accomplished by their imitating and obeying Jesus (who is the perfect image of God) as His disciples through the supernatural empowerment and enlightenment of the Holy Spirit.

Jesus-Style Disciple Making. Imitating and obeying Jesus as His disciple begins (but does not end) with specifically learning and then keeping the words, teachings, commands, and example He gave during His earthly ministry. Someone cannot imitate and obey someone without knowing what they said and did.

These first three principles ensure that the disciples we make are truly disciples of Jesus who imitate and obey Him, and they know why they must imitate and obey Him. These three principles then lead to the fourth principle of discipleship: the environment in which disciples of Jesus are to be taught to imitate and obey Him:

Biblical Discipleship in a Relational Environment. Being conformed to the image of Jesus by imitating and obeying Him as His disciple is not a passive process but an active and interactive process that occurs within a relational environment. Jesus established and demonstrated such a relational environment during His earthly ministry.

But what does being relational have to do with *theosis* through discipleship?

Be Fruitful

After the Bible introduced mankind as created in the image of God, Adam and Eve received two commands: "Be fruitful and increase in number; fill the earth and subdue it" (Gen. 1:28). Within the first command is the implicit command to be relational. Therefore, being relational with other humans is an essential expression and fulfillment of the image of God in which mankind was created. However, while created in the image of God, mankind is not trinitarian and therefore lacks the ability to be relational within themselves. Mankind can only fulfill this aspect of the image of God within them by connecting to God and with other human beings.

As they were relational, Adam and Eve would have reproduced and filled the earth with God's image as well as His glory. However, in Genesis 3, the woman's relationship with her children and the relationship with her mate were both cursed with pain and frustration because of the fall. In the fall, mankind lost the ability to keep God's commands to fill the earth and subdue it perfectly (Gen. 3:16–19). Instead of reproducing God's perfect image, Adam and Eve reproduced their own fallen image (Gen. 5:3).

However, as part of the restoration of the image of God within those who imitate Him, Jesus demonstrated making disciples in relational environments and through personal relationships. Jim Putman wrote (I recommend reading all of Jim's books):

> Jesus not only told us to make disciples but also gave us a model to follow in doing so. I believe that most Christians have divorced the teachings of Jesus from the methods of Jesus, and yet they expect the results of Jesus. I believe his methods are just as divine as his teachings. He showed us that the fundamental methodology in making disciples is relationships grounded in truth and love. Jesus is the greatest disciple maker in history, and his way works. Discipleship is the emphasis. Relationships are the method. Jesus invited people into relationships with himself; he loved them and in the process showed them how to follow God. His primary method was life-on-life.[25]

This of course seems completely logical, but the concept was completely new to me. My experience taught me the Bible was cold and boring. The relationship building happened when we weren't studying the Bible; it happened when we were busy playing money-ball or having fun in other ways. We had compartmentalized being taught how to live by Scripture in a box all by itself that didn't touch our real lives and relationships.

After I attended a *DiscipleShift* conference at Jim Putman's church to see if what they were proposing was possible, I wanted to do more than just study discipleship. I wanted to be fruitful and produce more disciples of Jesus. So my wife and I began a small group, and I began to have conversations with everyone I knew about what it meant to be a disciple of Jesus. I assumed that because I lived in a Jesus-saturated culture, everyone would be as excited as I was to learn what was wrong with our churches. I was greatly mistaken.

Of Whom or What Are You Making Disciples?

I discovered several harsh truths. First, I learned that relational discipleship can be misused to make disciples of something or someone other than Jesus. In the first century, the Pharisees made disciples of themselves, their traditions, and their theology in relational environments using Scripture just as Jesus did (Matt. 23:15; Luke 5:33; Acts 22:3). Even churches that generally hold to orthodox Christian theology can make disciples of something other than Jesus in relational environments using Scripture (like my church did). Ultimately, all churches make disciples of something or someone.

You might think, *Well, they aren't using Scripture; they are twisting Scripture!* and you would be right. But that is my point. Before convincing churches and church leaders that they need to make disciples of Jesus in relational environments, we need to establish clearly what a disciple of Jesus is, as well as the goal of being one. Otherwise, we might be empowering misled church leaders with a tool to make disciples of someone or something else under the guise of making disciples of Jesus.

If I were to ask a church member if they are a disciple of Jesus and if their church makes disciples of Jesus in relational environments, they would probably answer

"Yes!" even though the lives of those "disciples" would prove otherwise. You can play a game with a ball and a bat on a softball field and not truly play a game of softball. By the same token, you can teach Scripture in a relational environment and not make disciples of Jesus.

But at the same time, the only place you can play a real game of softball is on a softball field. And by the same token, the only place you can make disciples of Jesus is biblical discipleship within a relational environment. Just because churches and cults have misused relational discipleship, we cannot abandon it.

As disciples of Jesus, we must not only obey Him but also imitate Him as much as possible in our culture and context. And if we look closely at the ministry of Jesus, He interacted with His disciples differently than He did with the crowd:

- "Jesus spoke all these things to the crowd in parables; he did not say anything to them without using a parable" (Matt. 13:34).
- "[Jesus] did not say anything to them without using a parable. But when he was alone with his own disciples, he explained everything" (Mark 4:34).
- "Then [Jesus] looked at those seated in a circle around him and said, 'Here are my mother and my brothers! Whoever does God's will is my brother and sister and mother'" (Mark 3:34–35).
- "As Jesus and his disciples were on their way, he came to a village where a woman named Martha

opened her home to him. She had a sister called Mary, who sat at the Lord's feet listening to what he said" (Luke 10:38–39).

- "When they came to Jesus, they found the man from whom the demons had gone out, sitting at Jesus' feet, dressed and in his right mind" (Luke 8:35).

In case you missed it, being alone with Jesus, sitting with Jesus, or sitting at His feet is relational discipleship. Thus, because Jesus made disciples in relational environments, and His way of disciple making is the best, we also should seek to make disciples in relational environments. Ultimately, relational discipleship is the environment in which God ordained spiritual development into the image of Jesus to occur. Only in extreme cases, such as solitary imprisonment, would it possibly occur otherwise. For the rest of us, we can't be conformed to the image of Jesus outside of relational discipleship. Either we engage in relational discipleship, or we do not imitate Jesus as His disciple.

But understanding and teaching re-creation into the image of God is how we ensure the disciples we make are disciples of Jesus. Just as Adam and Eve were to be relational and thereby produce more image bearers of God, disciples of Jesus are to make disciples who are recreated into the image of God through relational environments. Understanding that the end goal of relational discipleship is re-creation into the image of God ensures that our relational environments have a specific purpose and a measurable outcome. Either the people we are discipling are conformed to the image of Jesus, or we are not making disciples of Jesus.

How *Theosis* Influences Evangelism

Growing up in the evangelical church, I learned that evangelism was all about saving people from hell. Emotionally, I completely understand the sentiment; no one wants their loved ones to go to hell. However, because we want so badly to save people from hell, we often make it as easy as possible to get "saved." Often, this results in the Great Commission being reduced to merely convincing people to confess that they are sinners, repent (without truly understanding the implications of that word), and believe in Jesus. We then hope that they live a better life and even attend church; but no matter what, they will go to heaven because they believe in Jesus.

But the Great Commission of Jesus is completely different from that. Jesus commanded us to make disciples, which means we are to help recreate people into His image through imitating and obeying Him. And just in case we misunderstood what He meant by "make disciples," Jesus reiterated that we are to teach them to keep everything He commanded (Matt. 28:19–20).

When we understand *theosis* through discipleship, we see why Jesus wants us to make disciples who imitate Him and keep His commands instead of just getting people "saved" from hell. Jesus' mission is not just to rescue people from hell but also to redeem the image of God within them through their being recreated into His image so they might render unto God the glory He is due. Isaiah wrote to this end:

> Bring my sons from afar and my daughters from the ends of the earth—everyone who is called by my name, whom I created for my glory, whom I formed and made. (Isa. 43:6–7)

As we have seen in other passages (such as Hebrew 2:10, which quotes this passage from Isaiah), being sons and daughters of God is a reference to being recreated into the image of God through imitating and obeying Jesus. Even in the Old Testament, the command is to go to the ends of the earth and teach those who would listen to bring glory to God through being recreated into His image—not to go and try to save them from hell.

Tozer wrote one of my favorite quotes on this subject, and it will probably offend someone:

> What a bunch of unworthy people we evangelicals have become, daring to stand up on our feet and preach to an intelligent audience that the essence, the final purpose and the cause of Christ is to save us from hell. How stupid can we get and still claim to be followers of Christ. . . . What a cheap, across-the-counter commercial kind of Christianity that says, "I was in debt, and Christ came and paid that debt." Sure, He did, but why emphasize that? "I

was on my way to hell and Jesus stopped me and saved me." Sure, He did, but that is not the thing to emphasize. What we need to emphasize is that God has saved us to make us like His Son. His purpose is to catch us on our wild race to hell, turn us around because He knows us, bring judgement on the old self and then create a new self within us, which is Jesus Christ.[26]

I have often wondered what the original audience thought when they heard Tozer's words. Did they listen to him? Were they offended by him calling them "stupid?" Did they understand what he was trying to tell them? Or did they miss it? But how would our evangelism look different if we thought mainly in terms of people being recreated into the image of God rather than saving them from hell?

Follow Him

When I went back and read the Gospels every day after being taught about discipleship, a surprising thing I discovered was how often Jesus invited people to follow Him and become His disciples. That is how Jesus invited people to salvation, not by asking them to believe in Him and say a prayer. In the Gospels, salvation is impossible outside of accepting Jesus' invitation to follow and imitate Him as His disciple.

Therefore, when we engage in evangelism, we are not simply asking sinners if they want to have their sins

Recreated to Be like God

forgiven and go to heaven when they die; instead, we are asking them if they want to render unto God the glory He is due by being recreated into the image of God He originally created them to be. We are asking them to commit to imitating and obeying Jesus as His disciple in order to accomplish that goal.

But what about "confessing and repenting of their sins"? What about "believing Jesus died on the cross for their sins"? Ask yourself, *Wouldn't they have to make those decisions to also make the decision to imitate and obey Jesus as His disciple?* People would have no reason to sacrifice everything to follow Jesus as His disciples if they did not also accept that they were sinners, that Jesus paid the price for their sins, and that they were turning from those sins to follow Him.

However, what we have allowed far too often in the American evangelical church is people confessing and (supposedly) repenting of their sins and accepting Jesus' payment for their sins, without being willing to imitate and obey Him as His disciple. Somehow, we have separated these into unique concepts in a way that Scripture never does.

Paul famously wrote, "If you declare with your mouth, 'Jesus is Lord,' and believe in your heart that God raised him from the dead, you will be saved" (Rom. 10:9). However, this must be taken within the context of what Jesus said, "Why do you call me, 'Lord, Lord,' and do not do what I say?" (Luke 6:46). In other words, you can't declare "Jesus is Lord" without also doing what He said to do—or He's not your Lord.

Most true believers in America probably have friends or family members whom they know are lost, but they don't know how to share the gospel with them because those friends and family members have only heard the watered-down version of the gospel and have rejected it. But have they ever heard about being recreated into the image of God through imitating and obeying Jesus as His disciple? Maybe they haven't believed because they've never been told what they are truly being asked to believe? Perhaps we need to go back and present to them the story Scripture teaches about the image of God they were originally created to be and how it can be restored through imitating and obeying Jesus as His disciple. More importantly, perhaps we need to imitate and obey Jesus in front of them so they can see what it looks like for a disciple of Jesus to be recreated into the image of God.

This then is also how we now keep the command, "Be fruitful and multiple" as image bearers of God. As we invite and teach people to imitate and obey Jesus as His disciple in relationships, we multiply the image of God across the face of the earth. And as the image of God spreads across the earth, the glory of God magnifies and increases. By making disciples of Jesus who imitate and obey Him in relational environments, we keep one of the original functions of the image of God: multiplication.

6

NO EXCUSES

From this time many of his disciples turned back
and no longer followed him. "You do not want
to leave too, do you?" Jesus asked the Twelve.
Simon Peter answered him, "Lord, to whom shall
we go? You have the words of eternal life."

— JOHN 6:66–68

The game of money-ball we played as kids came to my mind again recently when I watched the movie *Moneyball*, which is based on the true story of how Billy Beane (general manager of the Oakland Athletics) and Peter Brand (a Yale-educated economist) used statistics to revolutionize both how baseball players are hired and how they play the game. In the movie, Peter Brand argued:

> There is an epidemic failure within the game to understand what is really happening. . . . People who run ball clubs think in terms of buying players. Your goal shouldn't be to buy players; your goal should be to buy wins. And in order

to buy wins, you need to buy runs. . . . What I see is an imperfect understanding of where runs come from.[27]

Let me reword that to apply to churches:

There is an epidemic failure within churches to understand what is really happening. Pastors think in terms of making Christians. But your goal shouldn't be to make Christians, your goal should be to make disciples of Jesus who imitate and obey Him. What I see is an imperfect understanding of what a disciple of Jesus is and how one is made.

As I began to understand being a disciple of Jesus and the importance of it, I came to terms with the realization of how far off the mark we have fallen as churches. As I also began to understand the concept of *theosis* through discipleship, it weighed on me on how much of Scripture we have failed to teach in our churches.

Moreover, in place of teaching believers to imitate and obey Jesus as His disciples and to be recreated into the image of God, we have filled the empty space with whatever we could to make it feel like we were doing something important in church. And even when we agree that we are supposed to be making disciples of Jesus, because we have unfortunately forgotten how to do so in our modern evangelical churches, we often invest our time, energy, and resources into making something else—hoping it will somehow result in disciples of Jesus being made.

We attempt to make Christians, hoping they will somehow become disciples of Jesus. We attempt to make good, moral people, hoping they will somehow become disciples of Jesus. We attempt to make crowds, hoping some of them will somehow become disciples of Jesus. We make awesome worship experiences, hoping somehow they will produce disciples of Jesus. We make programs, we build buildings, etc.

What Are You Doing?

So what is your church focusing its time, energy, and resources on making? Be honest. Do you even know how to focus your time, energy, and resources on making disciples of Jesus who imitate and obey Him? Do you have a plan?

In my ministry context, an increasing number of people have given up on attending church because they have been hurt or disappointed by church members and church leaders. Interestingly, many would like to go back to a church if they could be guaranteed they would not be hurt or disappointed again so grievously. They don't expect it to be perfect, just not a constantly reoccurring train wreck.

But this is where it gets interesting: they want to go back and do church the same way it was done before, but with a different outcome. They don't realize that doing church the same old way is what caused it to be a raging dumpster fire that burned and hurt them. In their minds, a magical way exists to continue doing the same methods with a different outcome.

They think, *If we had a different pastor or church leader or if this person would change or leave, then it would work.* Meanwhile, the pastor, the church leaders, and that person think the same thing about them.

No one seems to realize the church must be fundamentally different in order not to hurt and disappoint people as it has over the last several decades. Not only must the church fundamentally change what it is doing but also what it is teaching. Because what a church does is a direct result of what it teaches.

Again, this is not to argue that the church must teach something in addition to Scripture; rather, that the church has not taught the full measure of Scripture. As a result, the church has taught and acted upon an incomplete message, which results in an incomplete church that hurts and disappoints people.

Get Up and Walk

In John 5, Jesus asked a man who had been an invalid for thirty-eight years what appears to be a stupid question: "Do you want to get well?" (John 5:6). Being an invalid in the first century was about as bad as it could get. Doctors had no modern medical conveniences with which to help take care of him. So of course, he wanted to get well, right?

Recreated to Be like God

The man's problem was the solution to which he was looking to get well. He sought to get into a magical pool that would heal him. The people at the pool didn't use the term "magical," but it was no different than believing in magic; they just spiritualized it by attributing it to an angel.

So there he lay, waiting for something magical to happen. As far as he knew, it was the only hope he had. So when Jesus asked if the man wanted to get well, what He meant was if the man would be willing to do something completely different to get well. But the man couldn't imagine any other way.

Then Jesus told the man to do something unexpected: "Get up! Pick up your mat and walk" (John 5:8). Notice that Jesus didn't magically levitate the man into the pool or up on his feet. Jesus told the man to stand up on his own two feet. Of course, Jesus supernaturally empowered the man to stand up; he couldn't do it within his own power, but he still had to obey Jesus.

Imagine if the man had said, "That's not going to work, Jesus! If you really want to help me, get me in the pool before everyone else. That's the only thing that can help me. That's the way we must do it!" Imagine if the man was dead set that there was only one way to be healed. But only Jesus could heal the man; therefore, only Jesus' way was going to work.

John 5 also gives another important detail about the pool at Bethesda: "Herein a great number of disabled people used to lie—the blind, the lame, the paralyzed"

(John 5:3). A lot of people sat around waiting for the same magical cure as this man. But the Scriptures record that only this man was healed that day. Perhaps no one else would have listened to and believed Jesus; they would have demanded that He help them get into the pool to be healed.

So let me ask you what might seem like a stupid question: Do you want your church to get well? Because a lot of churches say they want to get well and reach people, but like the disabled people at Bethesda, they sit around waiting on a magical cure—one that will never happen. Of course, they don't call it a "magical cure" because they spiritualize it just as the people at the pool in Bethesda spiritualized their magical cure by attributing it to an angel. But just because Christians somehow spiritualize something doesn't make it a real cure.

Instead, the real cure is to obey and imitate Jesus as His disciples and to teach others to do the same. This also means we must teach everything Scripture teaches about being a disciple of Jesus, including *theosis* through discipleship, even if no other churches nearby do it or if it makes our churches look strange. Or are we going to keep doing the same old thing and expect a different outcome?

What Will You Say?

Approximately eight years ago, I took an elective class on discipleship. After that class, I still didn't understand everything about being and making disciples of Jesus

Recreated to Be like God

(and I still don't), and it wasn't until several years later that I began understanding that *theosis* was the end goal of discipleship. But that class woke me up from a long slumber. I still often wonder, *Why didn't they tell me that first?*

But along the way I also began to realize that I wasn't the only one who didn't know these concepts. As I began to further understand them and explain them to others, I got to see the light switch flip in someone's mind, and they often asked the same thing: "Why didn't someone tell me that before?"

If we expect to see a disciple making movement in our culture, then we must teach and observe everything Scripture teaches and commands about being and making disciples of Jesus, including *theosis*. Scripture introduces mankind as the image of God and closes with mankind being restored in the image of God. One of Jesus' titles is "the image of God." Therefore, mankind being recreated into the image of God is an important Scriptural principle. Perhaps we should teach it as such.

To that end, I propose that we clearly and regularly teach and observe these four scriptural principles in our churches to ensure that we make disciples of Jesus who make disciples of Jesus:

- *The Image of God as the Basis of Discipleship.* The ultimate goal of the gospel of Jesus (and therefore Christian discipleship) is that believers bring glory to God by being recreated into the image of God that they were originally created to be.

- *The Purpose of Imitating and Obeying Jesus as His Disciple.* The goal of believers being recreated into the image of God is accomplished by their imitating and obeying Jesus (who is the perfect image of God) as His disciples through the supernatural empowerment and enlightenment of the Holy Spirit.
- *Jesus-Style Disciple Making.* Imitating and obeying Jesus as His disciple begins (but does not end) with specifically learning and then keeping the words, teachings, commands, and example He gave during His earthly ministry. Someone cannot imitate and obey someone without knowing what they said and did.
- *Biblical Discipleship in a Relational Environment.* Being conformed to the image of Jesus by imitating and obeying Him as His disciple is not a passive process but an active and interactive process that occurs within a relational environment. Jesus established and demonstrated such a relational environment during His earthly ministry.

Why those four principles? Those are the four things I wish someone had told me a long time ago. If I had a few minutes to go back in time and speak to myself, those are the four things I would tell myself, regardless of my age. Understanding those four things completely transformed my life. If I have time to speak to a believer or a church, those are the four things I tell them. Before

Recreated to Be like God

I die, those are the four things I want my wife and kids to know to make it through life.

However, after I wrote that outline initially, I quickly realized I had a problem. I hadn't been doing or teaching most of those four principles for most of my ministry. This is how understanding *theosis* through discipleship forces you to decide if you truly are going to be a disciple and make disciples of Jesus as prescribed in Scripture. I had to decide because I knew exactly what Jesus expected of me, and I didn't have an excuse.

Ask yourself these two questions:

- If Jesus came back right now and asked if you have been keeping His commands to make disciples who imitate Him and know and keep all His commands, what would you say?
- If Jesus came back and asked if you have been teaching everything Scripture teaches about being a disciple of Jesus, what would you say?

How would you answer these questions? Would you say that discipleship was too hard? That it costs too much? That you were afraid to teach *theosis* through discipleship because no one had ever heard of it before?

Personally, I can't come up with an excuse. Therefore, I am committed to making disciples of Jesus who imitate and obey Him. I am committed to teaching re-creation into the image of God as the basis of discipleship. I am committed to teaching that we are recreated into the image of God by imitating and obeying

Jesus as His disciples. I am committed to teaching that imitating Jesus requires knowing and keeping the words, teachings, and commands He gave during His earthly ministry. Moreover, I am committed to doing so in a relational environment. I will do all of this until I die or until Jesus comes back. Maranatha.

APPENDIX

The following is a list of free e-books and books for purchase from Discipleship.org to help you be and make disciples of Jesus:

Free e-Books available at discipleship.org/resources/ebooks/

- *Becoming a Disciple Maker* by Bobby Harrington and Greg Wiens
- *Revisiting the Master Plan of Evangelism* by Robert Coleman and Bobby Harrington
- *Disciple Making Metrics* by Dann Spader
- *Multiplying Disciples* by Winfield Bevins
- *Revival Starts Here Primer* by Dave Clayton
- *Untangling Addiction* by Dr. De Carvalho, MD
- *King Jesus "Embrace the Mission of King Jesus"* by David Young
- *Stay the Course* by Brandon Guidon
- *Inviting Along* by Jason C. Dukes
- *Dedicated – Primer* by Jason Houser, Chad Harrington, and Bobby Harrington
- *Fill Your Seats* by Regi Campbell

- *The Kingdom Unleashed* by Jerry Trousdale and Glenn Sunshine
- *Discipleship Is the Core Mission of the Church* by Bobby Harrington
- *Evangelism or Discipleship?* by Bill Hull and Bobby Harrington
- *Leaving a Legacy* by Bobby Harrington
- *The Discipleship Gospel Primer* by Bill Hull and Ben Sobels
- *Invest in a Few* by Craig Etheredge
- *Beyond Accountability* by Nate Larkin

Books for Purchase at discipleship.org/resources/books/

- *The Revolutionary Disciple* by Chad Harrington and Jim Putman
- *Disciple-Making Culture* by Brandon Guindon
- *Revival Starts Here* by Dave Clayton
- *The Discipleship Gospel* by Ben Sobels and Bill Hull
- *The Discipleship Gospel Workbook* by Ben Sobels and Bill Hull
- *Dedicated: Training Children to Trust Jesus* by Bobby Harrington, Chad Harrington, and Jason Houser
- *Discipleship That Fits* by Alex Absalom and Bobby Harrington
- *The Disciple Maker's Handbook* by Bobby Harrington and Josh Patrick
- *More* by Todd Wilson

- *DiscipleShift* by Bobby Harrington, Jim Putman, and Robert Coleman
- *Conversion and Discipleship* by Bill Hull
- *Stay the Course* by Brandon Guindon

NOTES

1. C. S. Lewis, *Mere Christianity* (San Francisco: HarperCollins, 2001), 199.

2. A. W. Tozer, *The Crucified Life*, ed. James L. Snyder (Minneapolis: Bethany House, 2013), 164.

3. A. W. Tozer, *The Purpose of Man*, ed. James L. Snyder (Minneapolis: Bethany House, 2013), 57.

4. Dietrich Bonhoeffer, *The Cost of Discipleship*, trans. Barbara Green and Reinhard Krauss (Minneapolis: Fortress Press, 2003), 284.

5. Tertullian, *On Idolatry*, trans. S. Thelwall, in *Ante-Nicene Fathers,* vol. 3, ed. Alexander Roberts, James Donaldson, and A. Cleveland Coxe (Buffalo, NY: Christian Literature Publishing Co., 1885).

6. Ignatius, *The Epistle of Ignatius to the Magnesians*, trans. Alexander Roberts and James Donaldson, in *Ante-Nicene Fathers,* vol. 1, ed. Alexander Roberts, James Donaldson, and A. Cleveland Coxe (Buffalo, NY: Christian Literature Publishing Co., 1885).

7. Irenaeus, *Against Heresies*, trans. Alexander Roberts and William Rambaut, in *Ante-Nicene Fathers*, vol. 1, ed. Alexander Roberts, James Donaldson, and A.

Cleveland Coxe (Buffalo, NY: Christian Literature Publishing Co., 1885).

8. Clement of Alexandria, *The Paedagogus*, trans. William Wilson, in *Ante-Nicene Fathers*, vol. 2, ed. Alexander Roberts, James Donaldson, and A. Cleveland Coxe (Buffalo, NY: Christian Literature Publishing Co., 1885).

9. Athanasius of Alexandria, *On the Incarnation of the Word*, trans. Archibald Robertson, in *Nicene and Post-Nicene Fathers*, 2nd ser., vol. 4, ed. Philip Schaff and Henry Wace (Buffalo, NY: Christian Literature Publishing Co., 1892).

10. Gregory of Nyssa, *On the Soul and the Resurrection*, trans. William Moore and Henry Austin Wilson, in *Nicene and Post-Nicene Fathers*, 2nd ser., vol. 4, ed. Philip Schaff and Henry Wace (Buffalo, NY: Christian Literature Publishing Co., 1893).

11. Basil of Caesarea, *De Spiritu Sancto,* trans. Blomfield Jackson, in *Nicene and Post-Nicene Fathers*, 2nd ser., vol. 8, ed. Philip Schaff and Henry Wace (Buffalo, NY: Christian Literature Publishing Co., 1895).

12. Augustine of Hippo, *The City of God*, trans. Marcus Dods, in *Nicene and Post-Nicene Fathers*, 1st ser., vol. 2, ed. Philip Schaff (Buffalo, NY: Christian Literature Publishing Co., 1887).

13. John Calvin, *Institutes of the Christian Religion,* trans. Henry Beveridge (Edinburgh: Calvin Translation Society, 1845).

Recreated to Be like God

14. John Wesley, *The Works* (New York: J. & J. Harper, 1830).

15. Lewis, 206.

16. Jen Wilkin, *In His Image: 10 Ways God Calls Us to Reflect His Character* (Wheaton, IL: Crossway, 2018), 16.

17. Matthew Bates, *The Gospel Precisely: Surprisingly Good News About Jesus Christ the King* (Nashville: Renew, 2021), 46, 51–52.

18. Bonhoeffer, 282.

19. Dallas Willard, "The Gospel of the Kingdom: An Interview by Keith Giles," Dallas Willard, old.dwillard.org/articles/artview.asp?artID=150.

20. Dallas Willard, "The Apprentices," Dallas Willard, dwillard.org/articles/apprentices-the.

21. Dave Earley and Rod Dempsey, *Disciple Making Is . . . How to Live the Great Commission with Passion and Confidence* (Nashville: B&H Academic, 2013), 49, 67, 68, 72, 73, 110.

22. Willard, "How Does the Disciple Live?" Dallas Willard, dwillard.org/articles/how-does-the-disciple-live.

23. Jason Dukes and Bobby Harrington, "The 7 Disciple-Making Rhythms of Jesus," Discipleship.org, discipleship.org/bobbys-blog/the-7-disciple-making-rhythms-of-jesus/.

24. Ibid.

25. Jim Putman et al., *DiscipleShift: Five Steps That Help Your Church to Make Disciples Who Make Disciples* (Grand Rapids: Zondervan, 2013), 33.

26. Tozer, *The Crucified Life*, 164.

27. Bennett Miller, *Moneyball* (Culver City, CA: Sony Pictures Home Entertainment, 2012), DVD.

Recreated to Be like God

ABOUT THE AUTHOR

CURT ERSKINE is the founder of His Words His Ways Ministries, which focuses on teaching Christians the whys and the hows of imitating and obeying Jesus as His disciples. Curt is a graduate of Liberty University and holds a MA in Theological Studies, a MDiv in Discipleship and Church Ministry, and a DMin in Discipleship from Liberty University's Rawlings School of Divinity. Curt lives in the beautiful foothills of Western North Carolina with his wife and children.